A WORKER IN A WORKER'S STATE

Miklós Haraszti, born in 1945, is perhaps the
leading representative of a new generation in
Eastern Europe: those who have spent all their
lives under socialism and remain socialists.
Naturally, they find themselves in opposition to the
authoritarian regimes which surround them.

Already famous in Hungary as a poet and
song-writer, Haraszti has twice been jailed and was
released both times after a hunger strike. His first
book – poetry translations – was published in 1969.
He was then given a commission to write about
factory conditions: he drafted this book, but it
was never published. Instead, he was put on trial,
fined and given a suspended jail sentence.

A sociologist extraordinary and a writer with great
talent and sensitivity, Haraszti has a promising yet
perilous career before him.

MIKLOS HARASZTI

A WORKER IN A WORKER'S STATE

Translated by Michael Wright

With a Foreword by Heinrich Böll
A note about the author
And a transcript of the author's trial

UNIVERSE BOOKS
New York

Published in the United States of America in 1978 by
Universe Books
381 Park Avenue South, New York, N.Y. 10016

Original Hungarian manuscript, *Darabbér*
First published as *Stücklohn* copyright © by Rotbuch
Verlag, Berlin, 1975
Translation of main text copyright © Michael Wright, 1977
Translation of Foreword from the German
copyright © Francis McDonagh, 1977
"About the Author" copyright © Michael Wright, 1977
Translation of the trial transcript from the French
copyright © Francis McDonagh, 1977
This selection copyright © *New Left Review,* London, 1977

Library of Congress Catalog Card Number: 77-088841
ISBN 0-87663-307-6

Printed in the United States of America

For
Danielle Jaeggi
Tamás Szentjóby

Foreword

A GLANCE is sufficient to see that *A Worker in a Worker's State* is a long overdue and necessary addition to the literature on work. Overdue, because it comes from a socialist country, and official socialist writing is habitually euphemistic, glamorizing workers and their world without saying how they themselves view it (it generally treats corruption as clandestine C.I.A. sabotage). The 'unexciting' thing about *A Worker in a Worker's State* is that its report and analysis culminate in a shattering banality: 'Nobody gets anything for nothing'. And all the talk about Eastern Europe's demands for Western 'know-how', when you stop to examine it, turns out to be based on little more than a pressing desire for skilled *management* which will get more out of the workers than up to now. It is, of course, an open secret that a Soviet functionary much prefers to talk to an experienced *manager* than to any Western sociologist or ideologue, whether 'Communist' or liberal, whether from right or left. It seems safe to assume that the lower efficiency of industry (and administration) in the socialist countries is not just the result of absurd mistakes in planning or too many bureaucrats, but also of far lower productivity. In other words, it is a human factor. In this situation it is easy to see that the aspect of détente which involves a Soviet or Hungarian official having a friendly chat with a Western efficiency expert over a dacha stove near Moscow or beside Lake Balaton will not be the most welcome part of the 'politics of détente' for the workers of those countries.

Miklós Haraszti's *A Worker in a Worker's State* is about the efficiency of factory work and its consequences for the workers. In this factory also 'nobody gets anything for nothing'. On the contrary, here too there are incentive payments, the absurd trinity of piece-rates, time-rates and supplementary payments; and the piece-rate per job is being constantly diminished, which means that anticipated output constantly increases. And 'The time we lose in asking for compensation – often without success – must itself be counted as uncompensated loss.' There is no escape from the cruel race between the hare and the hedgehog. The hedgehog is always there first, smirking or fulminating. He has only one face but many names: boss, foreman, rate-fixer, inspector. The workers speak of 'Them' and 'They', reminding one sharply of the Wallraff Engelmann book *You Up There, Us Down Here*. And when the bosses start saying 'We', things are becoming dangerous. It's bound to be 'We must make sacrifices', that is, 'You must make sacrifices'. Again, this brings to mind the pathetic appeals from our captains of industry.

Haraszti's book is much more than a factual report (a very good report). It contains various elements, some of which have so far been absent from the literature of work. It is first of all a detailed sociographic account of the techniques and terminology of work in a metal factory and of the relation of these techniques, terms and categories to that sacred something for which workers have to work: their pay, their living. This analysis maps out all the details, all the byways and twists and turns of the painful journey between work and pay-packet. What gives the analysis its clarity is the fact that it is also a first-hand account: in this case the person with the means of sociographic analysis and evaluation was down among the milling machines.

A third level of composition is not fiction, but is a component of abstraction which becomes increasingly abstract the more faithfully events and experiences are recorded. Detailed descriptions of particular work processes rise of their own accord into the abstract. If today, for example, you quote verbatim from the regulations of the German Army, you start being suspected of imitating Kafka (for example, the regulations for saluting: when walking, when standing, when lying down, when on a bicycle, when on horseback, when in a car, etc.). Or if you describe minutely the various bureaucratic rituals in government offices – the moving backwards and forwards and sharpening of pencils, the taking-off, polishing and putting-on of glasses – or the thousand tiny movements of a waiter in a packed bar, the description, while it is no more than accurate, becomes abstract and comic. So much so that the person whose work situation is described would find it hard to recognize the description as 'realistic'.

But there is something else in Haraszti, fortunately at the end of the book so that it can't be missed: a utopian, aesthetic and social dimension. This develops from his account of homers * and culminates in the puzzling remark that 'Most friendships begin with the making of a joint homer'. The beginning of this passage is almost lyrical:

> By making homers we win back power over the machine and our freedom from the machine; skill is subordinated to a *sense of beauty*. [my italics!] However insignificant the object, its form of creation is artistic. This is all the more so because (mainly to avoid the reproach of theft) homers are rarely made with expensive, showy or semi-finished materials. They are created out of junk, from useless scraps of iron, from left-overs, and this ensures that their beauty comes first and foremost from the labour itself ... If making homers were not such a fleeting activity, then one could almost claim that there were two schools: the first 'functionalist', the second 'secessionist'.

What we have here are terms from the history of *art* being applied to work. Try to imagine a union official, it doesn't matter who, launching the slogan 'Only homers fulfil you, brothers!', and then applying this slogan to his own union role! Government and Opposition (quite irrespective of who happened to be the Government or the Opposition) would be equally appalled: they would have to make an example of him. Non-alienated work, humour, beauty, pleasure are only for holidays. When they threaten efficiency, it's 'anarchy'. This is an issue on which Western as well as Eastern and Far Eastern technocrats agree briskly. And if you brought in the ominous word 'poetry', you would briskly unite not only East, West and Far East, but also

---

*A homer is an object made for his own purpose or pleasure by a worker using his factory's machines and materials. It is not an object made for sale as an additional source of income. The word does not appear in most dictionaries, such as the Oxford or Webster's, but appears to be the most widely used in England and America of a number of variants.

right and left. Is work to give pleasure and enjoyment only in the form of homers? What would become of the sacred object pay? 'My colleagues would think a worker had gone off his head if he came home on pay-day saying "I'm not bringing back a lot of money, but I have kept to all the technical instructions and fulfilled the norm."' There are lots of phrases in this book which have a terribly familiar ring: 'Comrades will understand that we can only distribute what *we* have produced.' Back it comes again, that suspicious 'We' used by 'Them'. The hares begin to run and the hedgehogs play Puss in the Corner. The hares may be in the majority, but the hedgehogs make the running.

After developing his account of homers, Haraszti says that: 'Were it not that [the] experts in production are also dispensers of our livelihood, in command of discipline and achievement, we would enter the age of the Great Homer.'

One of the accusations made against Haraszti in an official attack on his poetry in 1969 (when he was twenty-four) was his support for 'boundless democracy' and 'revolutionary asceticism'. If we replace 'boundless democracy' with the growing hostility in our society to even the word democratization, and 'revolutionary asceticism' with the rejection of consumerism – another idea long derided – we can see where Haraszti belongs. He is no 'agent of capitalism'; he is as unwelcome on our side as on theirs. He knows too accurately how the hares chase the piece-rates; how 'They', who keep saying 'We', see that nobody gets anything for nothing. Haraszti also understands that one of the results of détente in the East may be more technocratic know-how; and that the reassurances that factories really belong to the workers are empty talk.

That 'They' do not like such a book, 'those up above', over here and over there, is obvious. Their weakness and insecurity are revealed in the courts, though this is also a chance for them to demonstrate and successfully exercise their *power*. We over *here* have no right to feel superior about the trial over *there* of Haraszti and his friends.

Heinrich Böll

VISITORS to Eastern Europe are often struck by the extent of Western influence there, from Coca-Cola to blue-jeans. Despite national variations within the Soviet bloc, the effects of capitalism upon styles and ideas seem nearly as widespread if not so flourishing as in Western Europe. There is, however, one notable exception, which marks the different character of the States concerned: the influence of Marxism itself. In the West, since the mid-sixties, diverse forms of Marxism and new developments in revolutionary socialism have had a growing impact. Not so in the countries of Eastern Europe. There, the heavy pressure of official Communist ideology has acted more effectively to immunize those it educates from revolutionary thought.

In this respect Miklós Haraszti is original. Brought up since the Second World War, he has been deeply influenced by the Left of a similar generation in the West, especially the anti-authoritarian movement of West German students. His voice, therefore, is a distinctive one in Eastern Europe; its impact consequently fresh and sharp.

For this reason alone readers may want to know more about Miklós Haraszti: his promising, if unlikely, career as a poet-militant; the reactions of Hungarian officialdom to his work, and their attempt to suppress completely the manuscript of 'Piece-Rates' – the original Hungarian title of *A Worker in a Worker's State*.

Haraszti was born in 1945 in Jerusalem, where his family had fled to escape the Nazis. Both his parents were skilled workers and Communists; proud of their class. They returned to their native Hungary in 1948, after Russian hegemony had been consolidated there. Haraszti reacted against his parents' support for the Budapest regime by trying to become even more orthodox. He helped to establish a Vietnam Solidarity Committee when he went to university in 1965, after spending a year teaching in a rural school. His support for the Vietnamese revolution, while lively and independent, was partly Stalinist in form, inspired by Chinese polemics against Russian 'revisionism'. The Committee gained significant support in the university, and the police officially 'warned' the activists who were running it. Then, at the end of 1966, the police obliged the Committee to merge itself into the national Young Communist organization – the official arm of the Party – and Haraszti, with others, was expelled from the University of Budapest.

He spent the next year preparing the translation of songs which he selected from across the world. Entitled *Poets, Verses, Revolutions*, this collection was the first sign of Haraszti's remarkable talent. All the poems he selected had been either written for, or set to, music – from a Shakespeare sonnet to the ballad of Joe Hill, from Brecht–Weill lyrics to Pete Seeger's adaptation of 'Guantanamara'. The scores were included in the book in a way which allowed them to be used for instrument or voice, and the verses were translated into Hungarian to fit the music as well as the sense. Haraszti had already published his own poems; *Poets, Verses, Revolutions* now demonstrated his international awareness and a bold interest in form and audience.

At the beginning of 1968 Haraszti came under suspicion of belonging to a small group of 'Maoists', and he was placed under 'Police Control'. This is a special power utilized by the Hungarian State. Supposedly, it is a 'protective extension' of criminal sentences. In fact it is a mixture of surveillance and house arrest. The individual named may work at a job, but any other form of public life is forbidden: places of entertainment, restaurants, travel are all banned to those under Police Control. These restrictions may be extended or diminished at the will of the authorities: the police can impose an order at their discretion, without trial or appeal. The victim is presented with a paper on which is printed: 'The interests of common order and security demand that . . .' Name and details are then filled in. For Haraszti, the standard list of places forbidden to him was augmented by the further addition of university buildings and publishing houses.

Three months later the police arrested most of the small Maoist group, and its leading figure, György Pór, was sent to jail for two and a half years. But Haraszti had not been a 'member', but rather only a sympathetic (and critical) contact. Now that he had been sufficiently warned of 'the consequences', the police decided that he could return to university and his studies in philosophy and literature. So Haraszti spent 1968 and the year that followed normally. But it was not a normal time: the Tet offensive broke in South Vietnam, the May events shook Paris, Czechoslovakia was invaded . . . 1968 made its impact upon Haraszti, as it did upon so many others elsewhere.

In December 1969, *Uj Irás*, a literary review, published a new satirical poem by Haraszti called 'Che's Errors'. It contained six brief sections, each mocking a different kind of bureaucratic prejudice against the Left. The poem was attacked in the official Party organ *Népszabadság*, but Haraszti was also given the opportunity to reply. He responded with a defiant bluntness quite out of keeping with the Brechtian guile of the poem itself, and this was published. Startled, perhaps, by the audacity of Haraszti's comeback the authorities paused for breath. The debate meanwhile excited interest and established Haraszti as a controversial yet officially acknowledged poet. He was invited to a growing number of poetry readings until suddenly, in the middle of May 1970, he was arrested.

He was held for three days in jail on a hotch-potch of accusations arising out of the poetry readings and other meetings. The police claimed, for instance, that he had said during the course of one such reading that there were no soviets in Russia. On another occasion, in February on the centenary of Lenin's birth, they accused him of organizing a meeting to read selections of Lenin's writings without accompanying comments. In Hungary, the police are allowed to hold people for up to three days without initiating proceedings. During this time friends and accomplices of the suspect may be interrogated, and this process can itself be used as a form of warning and social punishment. After so questioning most of those involved with the readings, the police released Haraszti and did not proceed with charges. Instead they completed a document under Paragraph 60 of the Penal Code, which allows the police to state that a person has committed a certain offence even though they have not put him on trial for it. This document exists with its claim of fact, as an official judgement. The 'culprit' has no access to the condemnation. He may only appeal against it by demanding a trial, and virtually certain conviction. His official employers, however, may be shown it, and in Haraszti's case the University used the document as a reason for expelling him yet again. As he had just completed his degree, the expulsion served only to deprive him of his diploma and therefore the benefits of qualification.

Not satisfied with this, however, the authorities turned once again to Police Control. In July 1970 Haraszti received the now familiar form concerning the common interests of order and security, as did his friend György Dalos – another young poet active in the readings during the earlier part of that year. The police extended their restrictions over the full period allowed to them: six months. Dalos and Haraszti submitted to the order but decided that they would not accept a further extension for another half-year. When the police did impose such a renewal, the two poets sent a long letter of protest to as many officials and individuals as they could: Party organs, university mandarins, editors and writers were all circulated. The letter insisted that 'The police should not meddle in ideological questions', and it announced that neither of its signatories would in future obey the controls or restrict their personal movements.

For two months nothing happened; they went to the cinema. Then, in February 1971, they were both arrested, charged with breaking the conditions of Police Control, and sentenced to twenty-five days imprisonment.

The two had told their friends that, if arrested, they would go on hunger strike. As they were whisked from gaol to gaol, relatives and supporters tried to locate them. A significant number of intellectuals – including Lukács – protested. The prisoners were force-fed, but not maltreated. After the twenty-five days were up they were released, and Police

Control over them was withdrawn. The authorities had thus completed their sentence, and the prisoners had succeeded in holding out on their hunger strike, and in regaining to the full the limited freedoms of their fellow citizens.

Haraszti had used the first six months under Police Control to good effect: he had begun to work in a factory, to see for himself what conditions were like for workers in a self-proclaimed socialist state. At first he worked in a galvanizing plant. Then he went to the Red Star Tractor Factory – the subject of this book. His interest in the reality of working-class conditions did not stem from any preconceived notions of his society, and he does not believe, for example, that East Europe is capitalist in character. But although capitalism has been abolished in the Soviet bloc, it is also evident that socialism does not exist there either, in the political sense of open, democratic, working-class rule. The specific character of the states in this region is a *problem* which still calls for considerable investigation. For socialists living in these countries the difficulties placed in the way of such an examination remain nearly insuperable. Many of Haraszti's contemporaries in the West, by contrast, took an elementary step and entered factories in order to help organize workers or experience the reality of their conditions. None have faced trial for disclosing the conditions which they found.

This, however, was Haraszti's fate. Initially he sent the manuscript, which he finished around the end of 1972, to a publishing house that had asked him to write about working conditions. In March 1973 the publishers returned the manuscript, with a note saying that it was 'hostile'. The author then circulated copies to other publishers and friends. The editor of *Szociológia*, Iván Szelényi, agreed to include major sections of the manuscript in his journal – one of Hungary's main social science reviews. But the authorities were alerted. Haraszti was arrested; publication became impossible. Later, after Szelényi appeared as a witness during the subsequent trial, he was dismissed from his editorship.

Haraszti's arrest came in May 1973, and he immediately

went on a second, briefer, hunger strike until he was conditionally released from gaol on 7 June and could begin to prepare his defence. The authorities charged that to have shown to a single person the manuscript of *A Worker in a Worker's State* was incitement – liable to provoke hatred of the State. Circulating the manuscript to *a number* of readers raised the charge to 'grave incitement', which carries a possible eight-year jail sentence.

The trial was long delayed. After it opened it was postponed for further clarification. Then it was reconvened at short notice, on 11 January 1974, and a judgement was handed down. The author was given an eight-month suspended sentence and made to pay all the court costs – 9,600 forints – equal to nearly four months pay for a skilled worker.

Three points emerge from the trial, an unofficial transcript of which follows. The Red Star Tractor Factory itself is not mentioned by name in the book. The prosecution argued that this makes the volume a generalized attack on the system as a whole. Haraszti, in order to narrow his defence, claimed otherwise, saying that the book had a sociographic form but was a study of a single workplace. Readers, with the evidence in their hands, can judge this issue for themselves.

Ironically, Hungarian spokesmen unofficially took a different tack when the book was first published in the West. They suggested that it was now *passé*. Since 1972 when Haraszti left Red Star Tractors, the plant had been amalgamated with another. The factory, known before the War as the Hoffer works in Budapest, is now part of a company centred on the big Györ wagon complex. Formally speaking, therefore, it no longer 'exists'. Anyway, it is admitted, conditions were bad – although not 'that' bad – but now they have improved. Wages were low, now they are higher. In short, things are getting better; why make them worse by discussing what they *were* like? But the Hungarian title of *A Worker in a Worker's State* was 'Piece-Rates', after the incentive system which plays such a central role in factory work, as readers can see. The system of payments by results is not open to gradual improvement. And piece-rates continue to exist in Eastern Europe, compulsively driving workers on in their endless chase for a living wage. Haraszti used this point to good effect at his trial. He argued that, for his book to be taken as an attack on a fundamental institution of the State, the court had to regard piece-rates themselves as basic to socialism. The obvious discomfort of the court before this defence is evident from the proceedings.

The trial, however, served primarily as a warning to all dissidents in Hungary, many of whom were selected to appear before the court. Their courageous praise for the book, not made lightly before such a tribunal, was a warning to the Hungarian authorities in turn. An uneasy stalemate has since ensued. Haraszti's supporters have been attacked but not hounded; deprived of outlets for legal publication in their own country, but not deprived of all income from translation work or more menial tasks. Most important of all, perhaps, Haraszti himself has not been jailed, and he now leads the atomized life of a socialist 'dissident'.

Miklós Haraszti risked investigating his own People's Democracy at first hand, and has written about some of its effects upon the working class. It can only be hoped that his vivid account, with its truthful and distinctive socialist spirit, may soon be read legally in Hungary, the rest of Eastern Europe and Russia. His book represents a socialism which socialist countries can ill afford to be without.

Michael Wright

Notes

The Hungarian currency is the Forint and the
Fillér, with a hundred fillérs to the forint.
No exact equivalent is possible because of artificial
exchange rates and also differential rates of
inflation since the book was written in 1972.
At that time a take-home pay of 2,500 forints a
month was worth between $70 and $120, at
1972 values.

All explanatory footnotes have been added to
the text by the translator, and are marked with
an asterisk.

The translator wishes to thank Dr Tibor Csato
for his assistance, especially with certain
colloquial Hungarian terms.

A Worker in a Worker's State

PAYMENT by results intrigued me. I was struck by the contradictions in everything I read about it. I couldn't see how any compromise was possible. For example, in one newspaper, a Hungarian expert on 'management science' claimed that payment by results was the ideal form for socialist wages. It was, he said, the embodiment of the principle, 'from each according to his capacity, to each according to his work'. But in another issue of the same paper a veteran communist who now holds a high position warmly remembered a former comrade in arms who had been prominent before the war in the organization of workers' demonstrations against the Bedeaux system – the 'scientific' system of payment by results then in force. I read up the statistics and found out that most industrial workers were on piece-rates; I also discovered – but who didn't know it, anyway – that this chemically pure form of socialist wage-labour was the privilege of such workers alone: their bosses had to get by on much more antiquated forms of pay.

But what intrigued me more than anything else was something which, up until now, no one has ever seen fit to discuss in front of the revered public – which includes me: what exactly is it like, to be paid by results?

'I can see they've shown you what you've got to do, but as for making money, well, they haven't told you a thing about that.' M speaks without emphasis, as if to give more weight to reality. He is fifty-four years old; for the last fourteen years he has been working on a milling machine – determined to take home his 2,500 forints a month. 'If you want to do that too, you've got to learn the score. Right?' he adds. Exactly: that's what it's all about. I nod in agreement, and old M sums up: 'If you don't, with the money you'll be making you won't even have enough to go out begging for the air you breathe. Believe me, they don't give a damn about what happens to you.'

WHAT do we have to do? Between 100 and 120 people work in our section. We are turners, borers, and millers, taking up three rows of machines in the enormous hall. The next row is part of another section, of which there are four in the building.

I am one of our section's eight millers. It has eight machines. We work in two shifts, each man handling two machines.

The new machines and the old ones are pretty much the same. The oldest of all date back twenty or twenty-five years, and have two different sets of markings. On one side appear the words, *Manfréd Weiss Csepel*, in relief; on the other, *Factory Rákosi Csepel*, only this has been scraped down so that just the words *Factory* and *Csepel* are clearly visible. *

Each of these machines has been designed to take the full effort of one man's labour. 'What's so surprising? You're going to mill on two machines at once, and that's that. We made enough fuss when they first introduced the two-machine system,' M said on one of my first days. 'I'm the only one still here who used to work on just one machine. The others have all quit. The new men began on two machines straightaway. And, as for those who left, they'll be on two machines too, supposing they're still millers.'

Anyone who stopped beside my two machines and watched me work might well think that I've picked up all the tricks of the trade as I go from one to the other, regulating, tightening screws, pulling levers, throwing switches, getting everything going, then starting all over again. In fact, I'm not even at square one. Desperate, in a cold sweat, with a trembling stomach, I try hard to get a grip on myself under the pressure of working conditions and my personal

*Manfréd Weiss was one of Hungary's largest companies before the Second World War. Rákosi was the country's leading Stalinist after 1945.

preoccupations. This sensation first appeared when I began to feel that I was about to master the machines – and it hasn't abated since then.

M and the others know this condition well; they call it 'the nerves'. At a glance they see what I'm going through. And the foreman, who is always in a rush when he's outside his office, has also noticed, I suppose. As he hurries past, he tosses out words of encouragement – 'Well, my lad, we're getting on O.K. with those fifty piston heads' – but the way he says it makes me feel that if I bothered him about my pay, or about anything which concerned me personally rather than my machines, his face would crease into a mask of disinterest and rejection. Besides, even if it was something to do with my machines, I would have to rush through what I had to say at top speed. It took a while to learn how to put my problems in such a way that he rose to the bait. 'You've just got to make a really big deal out of anything that goes wrong,' my neighbour, a young turner, tells me. 'If you don't, he won't do a thing for you.' Sound enough advice, it didn't always work. The turner himself got stuck often enough to prove that to me. Basically, his approach worked only over minor matters, which were anyway the foreman's immediate concern. He would have to help you, however you presented them, so that production did not stop.

I work standing on platforms between my two machines, which are embedded in the concrete floor facing each other. The platform of the horizontal milling machine is a step higher than that of the vertical miller. And so I spend the whole day climbing up and down this step whenever I move from one machine to the other, to set up a job, or when I have to go round the back to change a tool or re-set something from the side. I grasped the secret of the two-machine system only when I got my first attack of 'nerves'. For during my training month the biggest problem was simply learning how to operate each machine on its own. They are not by any means the same. True, I mill on both of them, but not the same kind of jobs. For example, on one machine you might have ten pieces, each the size of a match-box, going at the same time, while on the other there's just one piece weighing seventy pounds. You can't go about these operations in the same way; one might take half a minute, the other perhaps three. The time taken to set the jobs up also varies. And then, for the sake of argument, the horizontal miller might be humming along vibrating quietly, while the vertical one is making an infernal din, racing round at full speed, spitting out sparks and red hot shavings. Both machines must be stopped at exactly the right time, without a second's delay, by pulling the correct lever in the precise direction. The controls and switches on the two machines are not at all alike. But the repetitive tasks demand a certain rhythm, and the different machines call for different rhythms. If I don't manage to co-ordinate them, then my work really slows down. 'It's like being the manager of a factory and a brothel at the same time,' said the work-mate who taught me how to handle the machines. 'But,' he added quickly, 'it's a bit more dangerous, and less well paid.'

On both machines the job has to be securely screwed to the work table. The horizontal miller has a shaft – running parallel to the table – on which you fix the different milling discs, equipped with sharp cutting teeth. On the vertical machine, the shaft is perpendicular to the table, and instead of discs it takes a milling head – a big, heavy steel cone with cutters at the bottom. On both machines, the table can be moved in three directions. When everything is set up, the job is pushed forward, by hand or by the machine, until it comes under the disc or the cone, which revolve at speeds fixed in advance. The end result of the operation is a groove from the horizontal miller, and a smooth surface from the vertical machine. Of course, the functions of the two machines can be switched around: if I take the long shaft off the horizontal machine and fit a milling head in its place, I can perfectly well mill a smooth surface with it; similarly, I can mount a disc on the vertical shaft, and thus mill grooves from the side. I can also mount a saw-blade, or some other tool, on either machine. These dirty, oily monsters are really quite versatile, even though the turners call them 'mincers'. A miller is quite literally a machine for chopping up metal: it tears, slashes, and hacks at the material, coughing out showers of burning fragments, quite unlike the lathes from which fly opalescent spirals.

In spite of everything, these milling machines could give play to imagination, inventiveness and application. But of course, only one at a time, this one today, the other to-morrow. It's not even that the runs are too big: a given operation rarely has to be repeated more than fifty times, and at the most a hundred. I haven't yet had to do the same job throughout a working day.

But, like almost everyone else in this workshop, I am on piece-rates. And that changes everything. Labour is turned into its opposite. Every possibility is turned inside out. Nothing depends on me. Nothing, that is, except my ability to put up with this inversion of the possible indefinitely. The only limit is my endurance, that is, my 'nerves'.

DURING my one-month training period, I was paid by the hour. 'A month is a long time; you'd be lucky to get such an extended apprenticeship elsewhere,' the head foreman said to me on the day when we settled my conditions of work. 'Good, in a month you'll have time to learn absolutely everything, and after that it'll be no good coming along and saying, "I haven't had enough practice", or anything of that sort. No excuses accepted. I'm going to give you seven forints an hour as a trainee. Of course, you don't have to wait until the end of the month; you can come to see me whenever you like, and I'll put you on piece-rates.'

These are the usual conditions for our section. I found that out in the first few days. A lot of men came to see me, and sometimes with little or no introduction they asked me what arrangement I had come to with the foreman. They listened to me in silence, and left without comment.

The turner who works next to me asked, 'Did he tell you how long your probation period is – the period during which you can quit without giving notice?'

'No, he didn't say a thing about that.'

'It's a week, you see. I expect they'll leave you in peace at least that long.'

'Yes, I expect they will.'

'Right,' he said. 'You've got it.' He spoke like someone who'd called check-mate.

Naturally, my eventual hourly base rate was also agreed at the very start. After an interminable preamble, the head foreman named the sum: 'In our factory, the hourly rate is a pure formality. Here, if you want to put it like that, we are on piece-rates; everyone earns according to how much he produces. Understood? All the same, we have to name a figure, but it doesn't mean a thing. You can ask anyone you like. Even the most highly qualified workers don't have an hourly rate of more than ten forints. Of course, your advance in the middle of the month is calculated on a hundred hours of work at the hourly rate, but at the end of the month you can take home money by the sackful. It's entirely up to you. All right then, let's say eight forints to start with. We can always put it up later on.'

'You won't be putting it up very much', I thought to myself, 'seeing as the base rate per hour is so low, even for the most experienced workers. And, if it doesn't mean a thing, why bother to increase it anyway?' Thinking of what I got in my last job, I asked for 8·50. He pulled a face, and went over his explanation again from the beginning; then he checked my previous wage in my work-book,* and settled for 8·50. 'Are you always so obstinate?' he asked. 'I've told you, it's nothing but a formality.'

Everyone I spoke to approved of the way I had carried out the negotiations. Each one had his own reasons. 'If you'd settled for 8 forints, he would have taken you for a sucker, and then you'd have been done for. The foreman just loves suckers,' a young turner assured me. He had just got his call-up papers, and so he was letting himself go, right, left, and centre. 'They need those fifty fillérs like a starving man needs a morsel of bread,' my milling instructor said. He checked off each point on his fingers: 'Firstly, it's a question of the average wage, or whatever they call it; they work that out on the basis of the hourly rate, and what sort of bonus they get for making economies here, no one knows. And then, it's not only your mid-month advance that's worked out on your hourly rate, but your paid holidays and sick leave, too. Not that you can afford to be ill with an hourly wage that low.'

There are still other 'advantages' to a low base level of nominal hourly wages: 'With an hourly wage like that, you think twice before quitting the factory. Say it's been fixed at 9 forints an hour, and you put everything you've got into the job, so you end up making eleven. Now suppose you want to go to another factory, where you think

*All Hungarian workers are obliged to carry a work-book, which lists their previous places of employment, their pay and why they left.

you could make 12 or 13. Right? Well, they might raise
you from 11 to 13 in the new place, but from 9 to 13 –
never. You just wouldn't get the job, even if they believed
that you were really making 11. You could find another
job rated the same as your last one, but you'd be very lucky
to get anything much better.'

All this seems a very long way off to me. For the moment,
I must learn to mill.

The miller delegated to give me instruction is delighted
with his prospects for the coming month. He is to be paid
by the hour, and, in addition, will receive piece-rates for
everything that we produce together. According to the
foreman, what we jointly produce can only be less than
what my instructor would produce working on his own.
The foreman thinks that my instructor's time will be
taken up fully in teaching me. But my instructor sees it
rather differently. He doesn't let me work on both machines
at once, although I'm going to have to do this eventually.
He sets up one machine so quickly that I can hardly see
how he goes about it, and then he leaves me to put a run
through. Meanwhile, he's milling on the other machine
himself, and he doesn't utter a single word until I've
finished. There's a hint of blackmail in his way of going
about things: if I agree to play along, perhaps he'll agree
to explain the odd thing to me, now and then. From time
to time, he knocks off early and asks me to punch his card
for him. In exchange, he's quite prepared to spend half an
hour telling me how things work.

But he's much more interested in chatting to me about
people than about machines. He's full of awe for those
who, he says, have 'got it all worked out', and he has a lot
of admiration for their most famous escapades even if they
don't succeed. His respect is not connected to success or
failure; it is the idea that interests him. I think he really
wants to be like those he talks about, but he doesn't have
enough confidence in himself. He is always worrying,
and takes the foreman's remarks far too much to heart.
When he's going to leave early he gets as nervous as a
soldier the night before a battle; he goes red in the face,

and tries to spot where the foremen are. From time to time, the others, too, get someone else to stamp their cards for them. But they don't make such a big thing out of it. They simply leave their cards in a friend's pigeon-hole. The following day, they say thank you. If the foreman happens to notice, then they think up some excuse or other. Quite frequently, they just give the real reason why they had to leave early. But my instructor suffers at the thought of what consequences might occur. When he is caught out, he goes into endless self-justifications, sweats blood and water, and keeps a forced smile on his face. Afterwards, when we are alone, he heaps scorn on the foreman.

At the end of my month's instruction, the head foreman receives me in his office. 'You're all ready to start? Good. You're a skilled worker now. For the next three months, I can, according to the regulations, raise your wage so that it reaches your hourly rate, if you don't manage to make that on piece-rates. But don't worry. We are sure there won't be any need for that. I have the impression that you're settling in very well. If you come up against a problem, then send for a setter. Skilled workers are permitted to call on the setters. But, of course, the more you sort out on your own, the better. Setters have a lot to do.'

His tone of voice clearly gives me to understand that it will not be appreciated if I make too much use of the setters. Indeed, it seems that he's only mentioning them at all to make sure that I don't go bothering them with my problems. But the others have already told me this when I was training. They were in complete agreement with the head foreman, even though they put it rather differently. 'You will starve to death if you wait for the setter,' M said.

SETTERS are workers who enjoy a special status: they get real hourly wages. Their job is to prepare the piece-rate workers' machines to ensure the continuity of output – or at least to help in the setting of machines between one run and the next.

I know the ins and outs of my machines, and I can set them myself. They are not automatic, and to set them hardly demands more knowledge than to use them. All the same, during my month as a trainee I did not come up against every sort of milling job. And then, on my first day on piece-rates, the foreman gives me a run I've never seen before. You can only fix this type of job to the table with a special device: the awkward shape means that I can't just put the pieces under the clamps, and I can't manage to fix them with screws and wedges either.

These special devices are left around the section, usually beside the machines on which they were last used. (Sometimes, when the big bosses inspect the works, the foremen run around between the machines telling us off for our carelessness, but piece-rate workers' minutes are far too precious for them to share these sudden passions for tidiness.) I don't have the time to go and look for the apparatus, nor to ask around the whole section. Anyway, I'm also supposed to be working on the other machine. I therefore go and get a setter. I imagine that it will be a simple business: while I carry on working on one machine, he will set up the other following the blueprint.

It's a lot more complicated than that. At the beginning of the shift, I'd noticed the setter strolling between the machines. Now, I find, I have lost all track of him. I look around, but everyone claims to have seen him in a different place. And all this time my machine is idle.

Finally, I find him in the inspectors' place, where, although it's officially against the rules, inspectors at a loose end compete throughout the shift to sell coffee at 2 forints a cup, in a subtle form of rivalry. I address the setter politely, but it's easy to see I do not arouse any sense of urgency in him. 'I'll come along and see you when I've finished refuelling,' he says, sharing the joke with the inspector who is brewing the coffee. I return to my machine. If at least he had let me tell him what I needed, he would have been able to bring the right equipment along with him.

A quarter of an hour later he puts in an appearance, weighs up the situation and makes me stop the other machine. He sends me off to find a milling disc from the reserve, and several precision instruments from the store. After a further quarter of an hour, I return. He isn't there any more. When he comes back again, he still doesn't have the special equipment, but I'm afraid to ask him about anything. He looks at the instruments ranged out on the ground and says, 'Go and get a size 300 depth-gauge too. It can't do any harm.' Then he busies himself with the blueprint, which, as I later notice, he already knows by heart. The minutes slip by, and as I rush back at the double, with my heavy boots clattering on the concrete floor, I see this vision of a taxi-meter which, with a curt tick, clocks up a mounting cost, minute by minute. But what is a straight loss for me is a gain for the setter: he's paid by the hour. I begin to hate him.

When I get back, he turns to speak to me as if he is my saviour, 'Let's go and find the equipment.' 'And,' he adds, 'bring a broom along.' We walk over to M's machine, and the setter points towards a heap of shavings. I extract the apparatus, heave it on to my shoulder, and carry it back to my machine. He indicates how to fix it on the table. Then I have to pass him the necessary screws, one by one. The wrenches are kept behind the machine in a cupboard; he knows that as well as I do, but instead of letting me work on the other machine, he asks me for wrenches of different sizes, which I have to go and fetch, and hand to him one by one. For about ten minutes, I manage to work on the other machine, but then he interrupts me again.

'Go on. Mill the first piece.' And he watches me do it.

I take off the finished job and we measure it. The first one through isn't always exact. The inspectors only give the go-ahead for a batch when the piece is perfect. I show him that it's a bit out. 'Oh yes,' he says dreamily. 'You should add another three tenths of a millimetre, or so.' At that, I can do nothing but laugh to myself. Add three tenths on one side; knock off two tenths on the other; exactly, that is called setting the machine. But I'm the one who does it, not him.

Our two setters are always engaged in this consummate art of assistance – and they think up all sorts of variations. Quite frequently, I need some tool or other, something goes wrong with the machines, the blueprint is obsolete, or alternatively reflects some draftsman's meticulous fantasy rather than the machine's capabilities: there's nothing for it but to call in the setters, although I always regret it when I do. Either way I'm the loser. I always feel that I would have done better if I'd tried to sort it out by myself. In the end, as we will never be able to communicate with each other, I take the decision not to call on the setters, except in the last resort. Even then, they carry on as if they were handing out alms to the poor; but I get the feeling that they are relieved.

At last, I have understood factory etiquette.

My neighbour, the young turner who predicted all these troubles, rattles off ironic remarks about each of them. He explains the situation to me. 'Look, they're just not here to make life easier for you. The bosses know perfectly well that the setters simply waste your time, but they don't want them to hand everything to you on a plate. And why should they be any more helpful? If you want to carry on with this, then it's much better to learn how to get by on your own. You've got to, if you want to make any bread: no one would be bothered if you don't even earn a fillér. When they fix the norm, they calculate the setters' help in the time for each piece. That means you get nothing for setting. They reckon you are skilled, but that setting is a qualified job. You can complain as much as you like that the setters might as well not exist; but up there, they are not going to worry. Down here, they carry on paying the setters because where there are bones you've got to have men to set them. There's no point in going on about it: if you do, the setters will take good note of what you're up to. They're all friends of the bosses; that's why they're setters. They are on the way up.'

I didn't really understand this last remark, and I told him so. By way of reply, he set me a riddle. 'Now you just tell me where, in your opinion, the older setter has been spending all his time these past two months? He was chairman of the local magistrate's court. On full pay, plus all the usual extras, of course. It's the same with the others. The younger one, who only became a setter last year, will be made a trade-union representative or Party secretary by next year, you'll see. The works manager was also a setter in his time. In a word, they're all in it together, so don't imagine that they're going to put themselves out for you. Even if you do everything on your own, it doesn't make any difference; they're still pinching the setters' pay out of yours. That's obvious. And you, well there's no way you can stop pushing yourself and chasing round like a mad man after you're own shadow ...' He speaks without animosity; dragging out his words. His eyes never leave the big piece which is turning on his lathe.

There are a thousand and one signs that the setters have really got their place in the sun mapped out. They are often 'in conference' in the foreman's office, sometimes even in higher places. No one knows what they talk about. Certainly it makes no noticeable change in their work. Sometimes, the younger of the two gets quite excited: with a mysterious look on his face he takes the trade-union official or the inspector (who is the Party secretary in our section) on one side; then, with or without them, he rushes into the office. In the afternoon, you don't often see the setters: no one likes to work afternoons, especially not those who are fathers of families. In principle there are two setters, so that they can work in shifts, but they always manage to fix things in one way or another so that they both work mornings only. The fact that there are two of them makes hardly any difference at all; if I have a hitch of some sort in the afternoon, I am completely stuck.

The worker who shares my machines was born in Szaboles;* he has three children. He has long since resigned himself to the situation. When he's doing the afternoon shift, he always arrives an hour early, and, in his slow and obstinate way, he starts to gather together all the tools necessary for his shift without letting up on the setters for a moment. The setters don't like him for it; indeed, whenever they see the chance, they make life difficult for him. If I add up the time which he spends on his work, without even including his endless overtime, I arrive at a really frightening figure: one and a half hours to come to work, and the same to go back, he lives near Pest; then the hour extra when he arrives early for the afternoon shift, thanks to the so-called help of the setters. That makes twelve hours in all. And there are many others who live two or three hours away.

---

*A district in north-east Hungary, one of the poorest in the country.

How do you earn money? Learning to calculate this is harder than mastering the job itself. Even so, some calculations are just as important for earning a living as the most strenuous labour. They give me money in exchange for my work, but after that I have to go through all the sums they have done to arrive at my pay. Otherwise I could easily fool myself. Neither the gleaming heap of finished jobs, nor my leaden fatigue, dry mouth and trembling stomach tell me anything about whether or not my work has been successful. I must learn to measure myself against the standards of the factory. I have to add up the value of months, days and hours on the basis of what minutes are worth, and I can hardly afford to be generous. They have already calculated each minute into so much for so much. The method is simple. They have converted my minutes into jobs done, and my output into piece-rates.

'Work-sheet' – that's what is printed on the form which comes with each batch. There is one sheet for each run. Once the inspector has checked them off, I get the carbon copies. The workers simply call the sheets 'money'. My instructor explains it to me immediately: 'The first thing to do when you get a job is to check the "money", and, if the people from the office haven't sent one down, you demand it straightaway.' Then, brushing aside the jumble of mysterious letters and figures with a sweep of his hand, he says, 'None of that need bother you. Here, these are your holy words.' And, with that, he taps a box at the corner of the sheet. 'That's the piece-rate. That's the only thing we look at. Take it as being in fillérs for a single piece; turn it into forints for a hundred. Just forget about the rest,' he says, rubbing the point home.

There must have been a time when he was interested in all the headings on the 'money' – for instance piece-time and 'work category'. But, like the others, he knows from experience that it is an illusion to think that the piece-rate depends on factors such as the time allowed for each item. 'Just ask them yourself. They'll go on at you until your head swims. Everything's fine on paper; there's no point in opening your mouth about it. But, if that lot up there want to slash the piece-rate – otherwise called "readjusting the norms" – they have only to give the order, and down it comes by such and such per cent. They just sit there with the rate-fixers, add, multiply, divide and rub out, and, at the end of all this, the piece-rate has dropped. But on paper it all looks fine; you can study it for as long as you like. It figures. Look, I'm telling you: just watch the piece-rate. That's all . . .'

I do study my 'money' and try to anticipate the results. When I have accumulated a good bundle of work-sheets, I take them home with me. At work, I don't have time to check the piece-rate, simply because I'm on one. And the race against the clock follows me right into my home. I have to rest for hours on end doing nothing, otherwise even the most simple multiplication becomes such a strain that my hands tremble.

It doesn't take long to realize that my calculations bear out my neighbour. The boxes headed 'Preparation Time' and 'Preparation Payment' are blank. And so the period allowed for a job (and the corresponding pay for it) does not take into account the preparation and setting of the machine, although this must take up my time even if the setter helps. My machine remains idle while it is prepared, as the rate-fixer knows full well. Just as I must know that if I want to do 'paid' work then – as my neighbour pointed out – I must also do things for which I will never be paid, even nominally. This kind of unpaid work is not just a miller's privilege. It is the right of every worker on piece-rates.

But perhaps this lost time is taken into account when the overall time for the job is calculated? After all, what is this 'piece-time'? How is it assessed? Why do the others obstinately ignore it even when, according to the work-sheet, wages are directly dependent upon it? 'Money', on its own, does not answer these questions. And so, for days on end, I put them to my machines, to try and work it all out.

I take the piece-time, as given on the work-sheet, quite literally: I follow the blueprint meticulously, and I run the machine at the prescribed speed. The technical instructions determine both the quality and the safety of the work. I only have to fix the speed, the rate of feed, and the cutting depth, then I'm ready to start off a run of fifty pieces. As soon as the inspector has accepted my first piece, I look at the workshop clock. Then, everything ceases to exist except the passing seconds. The machine turns at its set speed; only my own movements can gain me time.

After the fiftieth piece, I look at the clock once more, I pull out the work-sheet, and I begin to calculate. The sheet says: time per piece, 3·3 minutes; payment per piece, 41·60 fillérs. I completed the run of fifty in three and a quarter hours; instead of the 3·3 minutes which I am supposed to be able to meet, I have taken about 4 minutes a piece, and that does not include the time needed to set up the run. I have made 20 forints and 81 fillérs, and the better half of my working day has gone.

The result is more or less the same in all my trials: out of ten operations, two, at the very most, come close to the official time. (This is not because of lack of experience: some months later I will repeat these tests again, always sticking to the instructions, and the results will be hardly any better.)

My neighbour smiles again: 'What are you trying to prove with these alchemical calculations? You'll never earn more like that. While you did your sums, I made at least 10 forints. And I knew the result before you started: you're broke.'

The calculations I make at home show even more conclusive results. I establish that it is impossible for me to reach the norm given on the work-sheet. Even if I could – even if my output was one hundred per cent – I could hardly earn any extra. This is important. Because up to now I'd thought that it in some way depended on me.

From all this it turns out that the piece-rate is an hourly rate in disguise, or more precisely, a straightforward rate per minute: only those minutes during which the machine is running are paid for. None of the workers I spoke with realized that they were working for a dolled-up time rate; the deception is shrewdly masked behind the piece-rate system.

At first sight, the only difference between piece-rates and an hourly wage is that the latter is fixed. Those who are paid by the hour – not privileged workers, but those who actually produce – are simply held to a minimum output, and their wage is kept constant. But if piece-work is, in the final analysis, payment based on time, or more exactly a wage per minute in which one is only paid for those minutes when the piece is being manufactured, then the workers involved should rid themselves of the illusion that they are paid according to their output, and should ask themselves exactly the same question as those workers who are paid by the hour: what happens to the vast difference between the value that they produce during a minute (or an hour) and the payment which they are given for a minute (or an hour)?

Piece-rate is determined in the following way. The various types of work are divided into categories. 'Money' has a box headed 'W. Cat.' which means work (or perhaps worker?) category, inside which is written a number: 0·2, 0·3 or 0·4. The category is nothing other than a category of a fixed rate per minute quite independent of the agreed time per piece. In category 0·3 (which applies to most of my work) I can earn 12·60 fillérs for each minute of work. In the example I gave above, the piece rate is 41·60 fillérs: to work this out, the time allocated to each piece (3·3 minutes) is multiplied by the payment per minute of category 0·3 (12·60 fillérs). In this category, a piece reckoned to take 3 minutes is paid 37·80 fillérs, and a piece reckoned at 2·2 minutes, 27·70 fillérs. In category 0·4 (I don't often get that, and never any higher) the payment per minute is 14·30 fillérs.

The payment per minute, divided like this into categories,

is obviously converted into a rate per piece, which I can only get while I am producing a piece, and moreover within the time allotted for it. That sounds fair enough. When you work, you earn. A lot of piece-workers go along with the idea: very few think that it is because of the system of payment, rather than through a fault of their own, that they may make nothing for the minutes spent studying the blueprint, drinking a glass of water, blowing their noses, resting a little, or changing their tools.

With the discovery of the minute-wage, the following argument holds. Suppose that I carry out every operation exactly within the allocated time: my performance would then be one hundred per cent. Further suppose the impossible, that, for eight solid hours, from the first second to the last, I work without interruption, without losing even a tenth of a minute. How much would I earn then? Put it another way: for one hundred per cent performance according to the official time norms, what wage have they put by for me? That is easily arrived at: it is just necessary to multiply the payment fixed for a given category (which represents the wage per minute of work) by the number of minutes in a working day, namely 480.

If I work in category 0·3 for the whole day, produce each piece within the allocated time, and, for 8 hours neither regulate nor clean the machine, nor eat, drink, piss or attend any *ad hoc* meeting in the factory,* I will then earn 61 forints. If I have the good fortune to be exclusively on category 0·4 (which is never likely to be the case), my payment will then be 69 forints. As an hourly wage, that makes 7·6 forints or 8·6 forints respectively, rounded upwards to the nearest decimal.

So my experiments have the following result: if I keep exactly to the time allocations and to the technical directions as laid down in the instructions, the maximum remuneration that I can obtain for uninterrupted work, given one hundred per cent performance on my part, remains less than the minimum payment described as a

*Ad hoc meetings may be called at any time during work, without notice, about political issues or matters of production.

pure formality. The piece-rate worker who is unaware that he works for a wage per minute theoretically cannot assure himself of a full day's pay, except on the express condition that he does not stop work even for an instant. Obviously this is impossible.

More and more, piece-rates appear to me in the guise of a man who typifies the managerial spirit; a man who, up to this point, seemed to me, like the bosses themselves, to be severe but just, and who judged me according to the standards of a machine. Just: because he allowed me to pull myself up to the level of the machine; if I showed myself capable of a productivity comparable to the machine, then I received payment for each of my movements, just as the machine itself received electric current. Severe: because he punished me for being only a man; he did not pay me for the time when I was not a machine, during which I prevented the machine from giving birth to a piece. But my calculations around this one hundred per cent performance reveal a further characteristic of piece-rates. They are insatiable. They fix a norm, but take good care that I am forced to surpass it by making sure that even one hundred per cent performance is not enough to live on.

Anyway, the norms are not unreasonable only because pauses have to be taken during work; they are impossible to fulfil in any case if one keeps to the technical instructions that determine the quality of the job, and a certain level of safety. Another line of reasoning confirms my first alchemical calculations. The rate-fixers cannot but set a production time which demands a superhuman effort, since the whole point of the norms is to hold wages down to a level fixed in advance. If, for example, the sum of 61 forints has been fixed as the wage for a day's work at one hundred per cent performance, the rate-fixers are obliged to set the time per piece so that a minute of work does not yield more than the level fixed for the category; that is, the wage for a full minute's work. Even if the workers don't think like this, the rate-fixers are doing so all the time. Their point of departure is the pay itself – the 'incentive' of a danger to one's living standards – and not their experience of the true time taken to make a piece. Their stop-watches give a result which has been determined in advance, and this is the reason why the allocated times per piece, with very few exceptions, are unrealizable.

Piece-rate workers make neither analyses nor alchemical calculations: they learn from experience. Quite simply, they *know* that the time per piece is purely formal, that it is the payment per piece which counts, and nothing else. They concern themselves with only one sum: how high is the piece-rate for the job in hand? And how many must I produce to earn a day's wage? A sociologist would write: 'In the system of the people's economy, founded upon incentives, the norm plays the role of an indispensable fiction.' The man next to me says, 'The norm is a rip-off.'

I no longer think about the time-norm and other mysterious headings any differently from the others. My colleagues would think a worker had gone off his head if he came home on pay-day saying 'I am not bringing back a lot of money, but I kept to all the technical instructions, and fulfilled the norm.' The norm anyway can't be realized. There is only one way out of this vicious circle: every young worker knows it even before he stands at his machine for the first time, and so does the rate-fixer, from the day when he gets his first commission.

LOOTING

Safety Regulations for Milling Machines

1. Throughout working hours, work-clothes must always be worn and firmly fastened. Women must wear a head-scarf, men with long hair must wear a cap.
2. The wearing of rings, watches, bracelets, and chains during work is forbidden.
3. Before beginning work, check that machines are in good working order and that the safety devices operate. If there are any malfunctions it is forbidden to start work.
4. Jobs must only be carried out as laid down by the prescribed technical instructions. (The specified cutting speed, feed and depth must all be observed.)
5. Make sure that both the job and the tools are properly fixed and fastened.
6. It is forbidden to regulate tools, adjust a job, take measurements on or clean a machine which is running.
7. Whenever swarf is generated, protective goggles or a plastic face-guard must be worn.
8. In the event of any malfunctioning, the machine must be switched off immediately and the foreman notified of the fault.
9. Swarf may be removed only with the appropriate tools. It is forbidden to clean the machines with compressed air.
10. Machine hands must not carry out any repairs, whether electrical or mechanical, on their machines.
11. See that tools and gears are stored safely and are kept clean and tidy.
12. All accidents must be reported to the foreman immediately.

The Management

A copy of these rules is stuck to the side of every milling machine. When I started work in the factory, I was asked whether I had read them. I was then put through a sort of test. I had to recite all the points, one after another. I was asked questions about them in a relaxed, casual sort of way. The safety officer and I then signed the foreman's paper, which has since been attached to my personal file. If anything should happen because I'd not complied with these rules, the foreman would only have to get out my signature and everything would become clear: *I knew the rules, but I failed to apply them.*

In the galvanizing section of a factory where I used to work previously, and which was even bigger than this one, we spent the whole day plunging heavy pieces of metal into tubs of cyanide, chrome, hydrochloric acid, caustic soda, and other lethal poisons. We were paid, exactly as we are here, according to output. The safety test, no more searching than here, lasted five minutes. It did not make much sense anyway: apart from a feeble ventilation system, which made unendurable noises and draughts – we always unplugged it after a few seconds – there was nothing to protect our health. In spite of the rules, we handled chemical substances without using either goggles or the safety devices intended to stop the bottles from turning over. Who had the time to go and look for them? Our rubber gloves would always rip open just in the middle of an electrolysis and, to prevent this treacherous anointment from eating our skin, we used to wash our hands in hydrochloric acid after work. One man used to say that we were each entitled to half a litre of milk a day, to help avoid toxication. But he wasn't sure about that.

Before the test, they showed us a short documentary. 'The actors are great artists; it's really most instructive,' the safety officer told us, to whip up our enthusiasm.

And indeed, one after the other, the favourites of Budapest cabaret appeared on the screen. Ervin Kibédi played the part of the arrogant, disorganized, work-shirking malcontent, riddled with faults and quite unconcerned about the safety regulations. In his typical upper-class Jewish accent, he told what were supposed to be workers' jokes, rather in the way that he parodies car-owners' complaints in publicity films. László Keleti was the furious foreman, solely preoccupied with productivity. At first, he completely ignored the safety regulations, but later on – this was a bizarre touch – he fell on his face, hurting himself so that he had to go about squinting. In the end, he was converted. He put forward an angel-faced young worker as an example for everyone. This youth had charming manners, measured gestures, and demonstrated for all the world to see that even from the point of view of productivity it was best to obey the safety regulations. Our young hero argued with the foreman, 'Think how many hours of work are lost each month through accidents!' He was so sure of himself, our good youthful worker, that he made an ally of the manager himself, whom the film carefully avoided embellishing with any comic touches. In the beginning, and also at the end, the manager trusted the foreman. But the day when he discovered that things were going badly, he joined forces with angel-face to put everything right. It was even made to appear that the manager knew the individual workers better than the foreman – even though he was overburdened with work. He was carrying out research towards an important breakthrough, and this sort of incident disrupted his studies – but only for a few hours, we hoped.

The film went down very well with the apprentices. At each accident, presented as a joke and without any sign of real blood, they muttered all sorts of comments and remarks. They anticipated every *faux pas*, and laughed in advance. 'What a load of bullshit,' they said when it was over.

The fate of the twelve points in our factory was much the same as that of all 'twelve points' generally.* The first two are possibly exceptions, as no time is lost by observing them. If it wasn't for the fact that they are laid down as rules and regulations, even the young workers might well apply them, for they are just a matter of common sense. However, every section has its undisciplined, long-haired rebels.

But all the other points are our enemies, and a burden to the bosses, whose bragging about work safety increases in proportion to their distance from the machines.

The fourth point is the most important. Under the piece-rate system, and any other form of payment by results, its breach is both inevitable and tolerated. A piece-rate worker does not earn money just by working, but rather because he works without observing the regulations.

*Both the revolution of 1848–9 in Hungary and the uprising in 1956 began with a declaration of 'twelve points'.

My work-mates have long since given up the idea of their labour producing useful goods of high quality. They find it quite natural to be bound by special rules governing elementary matters of common sense, and equally natural to resist these rules, even when the price they pay is their own health.

But who batters his own head against a wall unless someone else is forcing him to do so? What immense force is capable of killing in the worker – who creates everything – the instinct for good work? You can, like the newspapers, believe that there is a point to a worker's life. But why should one be shocked by the indifference with which even workers who make a good living turn the page without hesitation when a newspaper article purports to give his life some other meaning than this simple desire to live well? 'You have to alleviate the *cancer*, but not cut it out.' Even the most well-intentioned say some such thing when they talk about the improvement of workers' pay or the relations which surround their work – they say nothing about the pitiless inhuman absurdity of paid labour itself.

When we work on a machine – whose output is basic to the calculation of our pay – and when we run it faster than the prescribed rate, then, officially, that is not called self-destruction (an inconceivable self-destruction which calls into question our whole universe) but 'cheating the norm'.

A strange kind of cheating which does so much harm to the cheater! If a fraud is perpetrated, then someone has to be defrauded. In this case possibly the employers, since increased production does not result, as they might wish, solely from the extreme tension of our nerves and muscles, but also from speeding up the machines.

If we received a satisfactory wage for one hundred per cent performance then, all right, it would be cheating pure and simple. Because we would produce no more than the one hundred per cent, but would do so with less effort, and the quality would be worse. But this isn't it. What would spur us on constantly to increase output if one hundred per cent performance was really feasible, and its corresponding pay satisfactory?

And so, when the jobs come out of the machine quicker than the norms lay down, it could well be called a sort of cheating, but for us, this only means – and that's what they intend – that we finish more jobs than are officially reckoned to represent an output of one hundred per cent. It's not a matter of working less. Exactly the opposite in fact: we work more to produce more in order to earn an acceptable wage, and this is possible only by cheating.

One might well ask: who is being cheated? Certainly not the bosses who in the final count can only be satisfied, because we produce more. The machines perhaps? They can take the pace. It is the norm which is swindled, only the norm and the piece-rate system itself. And suddenly, this norm begins to take on a concrete existence: it assumes the appearance of a boss, any boss, whom one then imagines one is cheating.

The workers call cheating the norm 'looting'. Millions of piece-rate workers use this word quite naturally, without the least trace of guilt. No doubt the god of piece-rate workers receives millions of prayers every day, which beg him to provide their daily loot. This meaning of the word is not to be found in any dictionary. Entries under 'cheating the norm' do not describe what the workers actually do, but mention bribery, doctoring the accounts, and so on, things which are unknown in the factories.

But management knows all about looting. After all, it is not just the workers who practise it, and live off it, but the bosses as well. If they fix my pay for a hundred per cent performance at around 8 forints an hour, then, quite literally, they force me to loot. Just how could their production plan be implemented if this compulsion was not built into it in the first place?

There is no need for them to go through all those calculations which I made to work out my wage per minute. All they have to do is to set the time for a job low enough, so that it compels me to loot.

Every boss banks on his piece-rate workers looting. If he sometimes reprimands them about this, it's invariably in a cautious, low-keyed, impersonal way, often with humour.

This usually happens only when looting too obviously affects the quality of work, perhaps when there are many more defective pieces than are allowed for in the calculated reject rate.

No boss would ever openly encourage us to loot. 'You can take money home by the sackful,' says the head foreman. 'It's entirely up to you.' Of course, he doesn't add that the hourly wage is a farce and the prescribed speeds can't be taken seriously.

M gave me my first lesson in looting. He said he couldn't stand to see the way my machine crawled along. 'You're not giving them any sleepless nights. If you don't work out how to make your money yourself, they won't slip the missing hundred forint bills into your pocket. Well now, what do you do when the setter has finished?'

I was going to tell him that I knew all about my machine, but he stopped me with a wave of his hand. 'This is what you do: you set it all over again. And if you begin without the setter, then forget about the technical instructions. He sticks to the blueprint. That's what he's paid for. But you've got a head of your own, haven't you? Well then, step up the cutting speed and feed the job through faster. Just make sure you don't blow yourself up. If you want to make a living here you can't let things run along smoothly.'

It's not easy. As soon as I start, the accelerated pace brings on an extreme state of nerves. My eyes are transfixed by the hail of sparks; my whole body strains towards the lever; sometimes I can't bear the tension any longer and pull too soon. The machine trembles and shrieks. The excessive stress on the material induces ominous knockings and vibrations. Their crescendo induces in me cramps and waves of guilt and fear. My torpid concentration collapses.

I concentrate on one machine. The other, timed for a different run, comes to the end of its operation; the milling disc hits against harder material and breaks, making an infernal din. The broken milling teeth shoot past my head like bullets. I stop both machines. My inner trembling gets the better of my hands. When this happens to experienced workers, they set about sweeping up shavings to master their impulse to run away. The unmistakable sound and the sudden quiet that follows makes the others look up from their own noisy machines. Their looks don't condemn and their remarks help me through a difficult moment. Slowly and unobtrusively, my neighbour strolls over and examines the shattered head. 'There are plenty of these in the stores,' he says. 'It's a disposable tool.' (At every production meeting, the foreman presents the same motion: 'The level of consumption of disposable tool parts is too high throughout the section.')

Despite their frequency, such incidents are treated as an event – and the news spreads quickly, like the word of a feat of arms among soldiers at the front. During the morning break after I broke the disc, a borer came over to me from the other end of the factory. 'I have heard the iron cry,' he said, with a broad grin. It turned out that this was the stock quotation on such occasions. He did not know its origin. *

Looting has its own excitement and rituals. Young workers, and those who are friends, spur each other on. The tense faces, the eyes half-closed through fear of flying fragments, smile for a moment. 'Go it, Pista, like you would the wife at home.' 'Go on! Give it one!' 'Is she turning red? What are you waiting for?' 'You've already shot your lot, Fonce, I didn't know you were such a weakling!' 'Hi, Laczi, where are you? You're hopelessly behind!'

But this does not save us from acute nerves, a condition which has nothing to do with personal irritability, whether chronic or occasional. Apart from the constant threat of accidents, the main cause of nerves is that not all work or every situation allows looting. We have to hunt out loot, catch it and hold it, plan ahead and get into position, throw angry rages on its behalf. Every day we have to fight for loot: small but in the long run vital battles, amongst each other, one against all.

*The line is from *Consciousness* by Attila József (English translation in *NLR* 37, 1966), who was one of Hungary's and Europe's greatest poets in the inter-war period. A level of irony is added by the fact that József, an oppositional Communist who took his own life in 1937, is today lionized by the Budapest regime.

All knowledge, skill, and application, everything needed for a good job, are put to the service of looting and so turned inside out. It is no longer a question of producing a good job of work, but rather the reverse. To discover every chance for looting and take advantage of them you have to know all the jobs your machine can possibly do, compare the piece-rate for new operations with the technical instructions, find out how to mount more pieces than the regulations lay down, learn how to step up the speed, and, in the case of multiple operations, find a way of getting right to the end of the series with a single setting of the table and a single milling head.

All this has to be done in secret and entirely on your own, because the foreman, the quality inspector, the rate-fixer and the engineer are all there to see that the rules are observed. They turn a blind eye only so long as you do not force your looting to their attention. The word 'looting' is not considered polite. But you can talk about 'good jobs' and 'bad jobs', which mean by silent convention nothing more than whether or not looting is possible. With the foreman you can speak quite openly about good or bad work. To him the rise in productivity through looting is an advantage: increased bonuses, and more prestige. Accidents and damage come under another heading. Our exhaustion, tension, and 'nerves' are not his concern.

M, for example, has a good look round before work begins and again during the morning break. He stops in front of my machines and scrutinizes the 'money' for my new jobs. Now he's no longer helpful. His eyes narrow as he observes me work: only if he is sure that my work is not 'better' than his, or that his jobs are just as 'good', will he spare me a few friendly words. After he's done his rounds he goes to the foreman and complains that he has had nothing but 'bad' jobs for days. 'You know the way things are,' comes the formal reply; 'bad jobs bring good ones.' The foreman means that if you want to get your hands on to jobs where looting is possible you've got to accept those which don't bring much money. The 'good' job is a gift, a bonus. The point of M's ritual complaints is not so much to solicit short-term favours as to make sure that the foreman knows what's going on. As they say round here, there are too many Eskimos and not enough seals. The foreman has a tendency to forget those who don't go along to see him regularly.

He also knows that, for piece-workers, 'good' work is not a bonus, but the only way to make a decent wage. A day without a 'good' job is a day lost.

'Nerves' get most acute when work is 'bad' – when there is just no way of getting the actual time for a job below the official time. At such moments, the more sensitive workers are unapproachable: they explode at a single word. The condition of the machines, the general muddle, things they never even notice when work is 'good', send them into a frenzy. The foreman keeps well away from them. M, for example, lets out a stream of oaths, takes it out on his machine, pounds the levers when they are stiff and lashes out at everything.

K is a peaceful man with a cool temperament. Once, he had to work for three whole days on the same interminable run of little turds: complicated jobs, impossible to speed up, set to a very short time norm. It did not give him any margin. Real bad, cheap work. He was sure the foreman would follow this with 'good' work. Instead, he got a batch which was every bit as bad, and also took a long time to set up. After he started, the inspector began interfering and made him reset the machine, once, twice, three times. Then, the moment the foreman walked past him, K, with a twist of his hands detached the milling head – a special tool which weighed at least a hundredweight – raised it in the air like Toldi* brandishing his milling stone, and hurled it on to the concrete floor, teeth first. Still not content, he turned over the milling head and started to smash the teeth with a six-pound hammer, sending out a shower of razor sharp splinters. 'You can't work with this fucking shit! If anyone says he can, I challenge him to come and show me!' When he had a 'good' job, he used such a milling head without com-

*Hero of a well-known nineteenth-century poem by János Arany. Toldi fought mightily against feudal coercion.

plaint. The foreman had the fragments of the precious tool carried away – it took two men to do the job – but it didn't occur to him for one moment to give K a dressing-down, or to make him pay for the damage.

'Nerves' brought about by the necessity of looting cannot be calmed by anything except loot itself. We have to stake all our inventiveness, knowledge, imagination, initiative and courage on getting it. And when this comes off, it brings a certain feeling of triumph. This is why workers on piece-rates often feel that they have beaten the system, as if they'd got the better of someone. But looting does not make the work any easier; it intensifies the physical and mental effort demanded. The time won is used to make even more pieces. If we stopped, carried away by the sheer joy of success, we should lose all the advantages we had gained. Despite this we talk among ourselves about our looting with an air of conspiracy, as if it was a decisive blow in the unending, daily battles.

M is decidedly proud of his reputation. Even the turners speak with respect about his looting, although they have a traditional contempt for the millers' dirty trade. He really does get up to some fastastic tricks. One of his favourites is to lay the huge, heaviest pieces on the milling table, without fastening them down, and to lean against them with the whole weight of his body while the table moves to and fro, and the cutters screech. Just to watch him sends cold shivers down your spine. A grain of impurity in the material, or a fault in the casting, and the insane speed of the head will rip the piece from between his hands. But if he doesn't do it that way, he will lose the two minutes to be gained from every ten.

L, who is coming up to retirement, has been given the chance of doing exactly the same work every day. He mills the gaps in between the teeth on cog wheels. Each piece has to be worked on three sides. This is how he grabs his loot: when he has finished on one of the three sides he uses one hand to loosen the clamps (which are anyway fewer than the number laid down in the regulations) as the table comes back at full speed and the spindle continues to rev.

When the table gets back to its initial position, he can immediately pivot the piece around without stopping the milling head, so that he can then let the machine carry on with its cycle while he tightens the clamp on to the new position. Is it safe to work with so few clamps? Does he have time to check that they are fastened tightly enough or that the piece isn't going to smash into the revolving head? He never asks questions like this. If he worked to the rules, in one fell swoop his job would be metamorphosed into 'bad' work, and he would have lost his 'living'.

Around Christmas time, we were made tragically aware of the way L worked. In the adjacent section there was an accident involving another miller who put L's pieces through their next operation. This worker also took advantage of the chance to pivot the pieces around. The milling head tore off the fingers from his right hand. The stretcher on which they carried him out passed right in front of old L's machine.

The foreman sent for the millers and gave us a little talk in his office. 'On the occasion of this most regrettable incident, I would like to take the opportunity of emphasizing to you that in our section we can boast about the fact that we have had very few accidents indeed. It is in all our interests' – this was his favourite phrase – 'to keep things this way. This scramble at the end of the year isn't very pleasant for anyone, but it involves all of us, because the final outcome will affect us all. It would therefore be a good thing if we kept our safety record to its present level, and finished the year without an accident. We must learn from what has just happened. You are grown men, I know, but you shouldn't be ashamed to learn. Has anyone got any questions? Now, please sign the minutes of this *ad hoc* meeting.' On the sheet of paper, you could read that the foreman had drawn our attention to the importance of keeping to the technical regulations, and the workers had registered their agreement. We went back to the section, and everyone continued exactly as before: including old L.

I DISCOVER a change in myself. My interest in materials, techniques and ways of economizing my strength is first coloured and then dominated by an obsession about making money. I surrender to an oppressive, unspoken but all-powerful taboo: never approach work to make it more exact, easy, enjoyable or safe.

One day, it struck me that I had almost come to hate the innocent, friendly and talkative woman whose job it was to give out the work allocations. Before my eyes, she split a batch of 150 pieces – all of which could have come my way – into two lots of 75. Actually, she did this only to ensure that the fitters received a steady flow of finished pieces from us millers. Two months earlier, I would have been pleased to have been landed with only 75 jobs of this sort because the work involved was particularly nerve-wracking. Every piece has to be hammered into position, and after every operation the swarf has to be cleaned from the surfaces of the clamps completely, or the next piece would not be true to measure. But since then, I had found a way of doing them three times as fast as the official speed, and the quality inspector still accepted them. That's why I was so furious when I learned that I might not get the other half of the run, and that, even if I did get it, I would have to reset my machine and have it checked all over again. This job has not become any less demanding, only now it is 'good' work and it is impossible for me not to like it.

When I have work of this type – and it is always more trying because looting inevitably means speeding things up – I can't help wishing, however monotonous it is, that it will go on for ever, that my cuts will be slight enough not to need treatment, that the worker who should take over from me will be sick so that I can carry on and do overtime, that no one talks to me, that nothing will come into my mind which might distract my attention or interrupt my will,

that I will have neither hunger nor thirst, and that everything will be exactly the same tomorrow. My basic ideas
have not changed (perhaps only because I haven't always
been here, and I won't have to go on doing this job for
ever?), but somehow I am split. In the showers, I feel guilt
as I recall the rage in which I repeated the same movements, minute after minute. I say 'guilt' because I have
discovered that this rage comes from the tension of looting,
and nothing else.

Of course, I have to do 'bad' jobs too, when I try to lose
as little time as I can; this sort of work allows you to get jobs
in which looting is possible, which in turn lets your wage
reach a half-way acceptable level. When I do a job which
doesn't allow for looting, all that I feel about myself is hate
and bitterness; my brain won't admit that even with such
work I should be pushing myself to the limit. I am easily
distracted because I only have to look at my work-sheet to
know that, at best, I am working for thirteen fillérs a
minute.

In the end, the only way out is to become a machine
myself. The best workers are very good at this. It is as if an
immovable mask was glued to their faces, whatever the type
of work they are doing. Their eyes seem veiled, yet they
never miss a thing. Their movements don't seem to require
any effort. They follow predetermined trajectories, like
inert objects under magnetic control. Throughout the whole
day, they keep to a fast even pace. Just like the machines,
they don't rush into things when they are feeling fresh,
nor do they slow up when they're tired. They give way to
'nerves' only when the proportion of 'good' work to 'bad'
is really grim. Otherwise, their behaviour reflects reality:
'good' and 'bad' jobs, 'paid' and 'unpaid' work, run
together in the course of a day. The benefits they squeeze
out of them and the wages which come from them are
equally indifferent to such distinctions.

In itself, the difference between 'good' and 'bad' work is
born of illusion, there are no clear criteria for determining
it.

After I had worked out the pay for eight hours work with

100 per cent performance, I told my shift-mate the figures I had arrived at. He was surprised and incredulous. 'I knew that you had to get a move on, and that the prescribed time was only there so that they could show something on the paper, but I never realized that if I worked honestly throughout my shift, at a 100 per cent performance, I still wouldn't reach the nominal hourly pay rate. Well, you never can trust a piece of printed paper!'

Particularly when jobs are of a new or unusual kind, whether or not they are 'good' or 'bad' does not emerge until you do your accounting afterwards. This is especially true if you are a beginner. Even with experience, you can never tell in advance just how 'good' or 'bad' a job is. There is only one thing that's absolutely certain: 'Don't stick to the technical instructions!' This is the only way to make sure that we don't miss a 'good' job. But experience does not enable us to work out our gains with certainty – just to make, at best, a rough guess.

INSECURITY is the main driving force in all payment by results – both piece-rate and contract work. It chases us remorselessly every minute of the day. That's why payment by results is held to be the best incentive of all.

The manifest coercion and dependence which characterize payment by the hour change into a semblance of independence with piece-rates. Workers on assembly lines, or on automatic or semi-automatic equipment, serve machines which they do not control, which run at a constant pace, and whose output is fixed in advance. In return, they get a predetermined wage – usually at an hourly rate. Such workers can only increase their earnings by stepping up the number of hours they work, by doing overtime. Within the official limits, their precise hourly pay is fixed individually: you get so much, and you, so much. The boss fixes your pay and he can arbitrarily increase it entirely as he sees fit.

The time-rate worker knows, therefore, what is expected of him and what he can expect in return. He does not have to make an economic analysis for the essence of time-rates to stare him in the face. His eight hours have been bought from him. The machine holds to its inescapable rhythm. It cannot be deceived. He has as little influence over the price of his working day as he has over how, when, where and in whose interests the value which he produces (and of which he receives a part) is used. There is little chance of his getting bogged down in details, and coming to see part of his work as 'paid' and part as 'unpaid', or to rate some of his jobs as 'good' and others as 'bad'. He does not envisage that astute tricks or individual effort might turn the system to his advantage. If he regards something as unjust – for example, his rate of pay – then, as he broods over ways and means of bringing about a change, he must either come to see the whole system as unjust, or accept it in its totality as a fate which says: 'That's the way it is.' Whatever position he arrives at, coercion, dependence, and obedience – the very essence of paid labour – are quite clear to him, however well paid he happens to be. Whenever he possibly can, he reduces his suffering. When he works faster, or infringes the technical regulations, he doesn't do so, like a piece-rate worker, to produce more. On the contrary, when he feels that his output is more than is being asked of him, he slows down. In a word, time-rates are straightforward: an 'incentive wage form'.

A worker paid by the hour knows that he can't demand anything; he has to accept that something will be handed out to him in the end. The piece-rate worker also knows about what he can't expect. But he is bound to believe that he can do one thing through his own efforts: make money. When he earns his pay, he thinks he is getting the reward for a private struggle. Every day, he starts at zero. Every day the mirage of limitless possibilities shimmers on his horizon. The forints that he earns are the spoils of a battle, involving something which appears to depend upon himself. Beside those external factors about which he cannot do a thing – materials, regulations, pay rates, controls – stands his own will. He himself works his machine.

It is not enough that the conditions are skilfully set up for the compulsion of work to take over. A totally alien flow of time fragments his life. His working day is disguised minute by minute by the renewed effort of will he incessantly squeezes from himself. His belief that in all circumstances it is possible to extract more money than he has been allocated is subtly reinforced. He does not notice that his will has been taken into account in a cold calculation, in which, whether he breaks through the set limits or stays within them, it comes to the same thing. His efforts only generate further profits and new demands upon himself.

Uncertainty is the great magician of piece-work. It puts life back into those details which the time-rate worker does not even think about when he installs himself in front of his machine: the speed of the spindle; the technology of the process; the pay. If a man on hourly pay feels cheated, then he feels that he has been cheated totally, absolutely, and in every way. The piece-rate worker, however, just would not start work at all if he began the day with a resigned, passive feeling that he was going to be cheated. For him the chance of something extra is essential. Of course, he knows perfectly well that he is being cheated. But his active participation in this trick against himself makes it impossible for him to see the deception; or to identify it with his conditions of life, as can the worker on hourly wages.

Instead, he has a sharp eye for petty discrimination, injustice or manipulation, and fights against such things in the belief that such victories can be set against the defeats. He tends to judge everything in terms of pay, and when he has a good month, he believes, from the bottom of his heart, that he is not the dupe but the victor.

If the time-rate worker notices that his rate of production is faster than it was two months ago he says to himself, 'They have speeded up the conveyor, modified the machine, replaced the tools, or altered the raw materials. It is up to them. I can't do anything about it.' But when a piece-rate worker discovers that the norm for a particular job has been tightened, he remembers that he recently increased his output in the hope of the temporary advantage of a better pay-slip. How could he admit to himself that his will was part of something that had been willed outside of him, and that what has happened has, in one way or another, been planned? He must look for another explanation and think about the instance as a temporary setback, an exception rather than the rule.

How much work do we do? My neighbour the turner, who returned from military service two years ago, claims that he has to produce a lot more now to earn the same wage as he got before he went into the army (and today with such a wage he can hardly make ends meet) even though he is still on the same machine doing the same work. Everyone else agrees, even those turners who are paid by the hour and work on semi-automatic machines. The millers are not short of things to say about this. M, for example, likes to talk about the Golden Age when he worked on one machine only. Or take his shift replacement, who once watched a weight-lifting champion on the television. When he heard the commentator enthuse that there were no real limits to man's prowess, he reacted: 'All these guys have to do is to lift up one milligramme more than the others, and they are covered with gold.' Warming to his punch-line, he went on, 'They certainly don't have to eat shit. But I am forced to push through twice as much, and no one thinks of putting me on the T.V.'

The real meaning of piece-rates lies in the incessant increase in production. The bosses do not have to impose it. It is enough for them to register that it has happened and then to incorporate it officially by changing the norms. Of course, there are sometimes abuses and injustices: occasionally management pushes matters and goes a bit too far in setting the new norm, even though the compulsion to loot would get the same result anyway. But clever management simply acknowledges the results which have been achieved, and bases further increases upon them.

The production graph is used to justify a revision of the norm. They could establish its trajectory for each individual worker, but usually they prefer to base it on the largest possible sample, taking, for example, the average increase in production throughout the sections, or that of all the turners. The calculation is simple. If I produce at the official 100 per cent, my output is 100 per cent; if I produce more it is more. (We are on a 'continuous', and not 'declining' piece-rate: this means that every piece over and above the 100 per cent norm is paid for at the same rate.) And so who isn't producing more than 100 per cent? The pay for 100 per cent is fixed in such a way that we have to make more. That is clear. So we always try to squeeze the maximum out of every job – if it is 'bad' precisely because it is 'bad', and if it is 'good', because it gives us a chance to loot. We worry about our pay, not about our norms – and you can't call that negligence. The method of production accounting does not allow us to follow fluctuations in our personal levels of production: when we check how we are doing we add up the wage per piece, but those upstairs add up piece-times – without allowing for the fact that it is impossible to respect the time per piece, or that down here we are looting.

Once a fortnight – or occasionally three times a month – we get an overall account, 'The Ten Day Bulletin', as it's called. Even if this gave us a breakdown of real times for each piece, which they would not dream of doing, we still could not extract from it information about our monthly performance. The computer only registers batches of work on the Bulletin in the order in which they are checked off by the administration. So it often includes work from the previous ten days. These bulletins, several pages long, reflect the great variety of work we do. The endless, closely printed columns of signs and figures come in the following order: personal number of the worker – that means me; type of work; time per piece; number of pieces; piece-rate; and finally at the bottom, the total piece wage. If we want to get an idea of what our production graph looks like, then we must multiply the time per piece by the number of pieces and then, on the basis of results from three successive bulletins, reach a total and compare it with the hours of work which we put in during the month. The bulletin is obliging: it indicates the sum total of wages per piece. In theory, therefore, assuming that one has kept all one's 'money' and laboriously computed it, it is at least possible to check if they have cheated us on a run and if they have accounted for all the work done.

And what if each of us calculated his output as soon as he finished each run, by multiplying the number of pieces by the time per piece? Well, we would only lose the few minutes gained by looting.

So we carry on looting, blindly, with this inevitable result: the pursuit of maximum gain forces the pay per piece downwards. This comes about through the progressive reduction of the time-rate per piece, and it prevents us from controlling our rate of production, which, of course, is incessantly stepped up. For the same wage we do more and more work, while the cost of living is always going up; to have the same amount in real terms, it is always necessary to do an ever-increasing amount of work.

The foremen and the rate-fixers draw up the production graphs, but they rarely tell the workers the relevant figures, not even in the course of the obligatory quarterly meetings about productivity. If they do, it's usually a bad sign for us. It means that the increase in productivity has been sufficient to justify the introduction of new norms. When questions relating to scales of production are announced, it means that an increase in the norms will certainly follow.

Many have previous experience of other systems of payment, and from time to time there are heated discussions about which is best. Everyone agrees that they would not choose an hourly rate unless it guaranteed that they would be paid at least their present earnings. The slight difference between the take-home pay of the hourly wage worker and of those on piece-rates is enough for them voluntarily to accept endless increases in the rate of production – for production piece-rates really are an 'incentive' discovery.

There is a running argument over different forms of piece-rates. One party, the party of the big looters, holds that piece-rates help those who help themselves, and that this form of pay does enable one occasionally to get together a really tidy sum. Others favour the contract system. True, it seems to make it more difficult to reach 100 per cent; nevertheless it seems to give more initial control over production, and this leads to a feeling of being better armed against increases in the norm, and of greater ease and security.

These discussions die down for a good while when they let us know the figures for overall production, though this happens very rarely. Then the various protagonists are reduced to silence. The most daring discover that they have only just reached what was fixed for them by destiny; the heroes of looting feel the rope around their neck.

We learn a new lesson about the logic of wage labour, a lesson which can be put like this: a man who creates wealth is compelled to work in a way which destroys the quality of that which he produces, and his own health as well; simultaneously, he is forbidden to work in this way, as if he would ever choose to do so of his own free will.

The idlest and most far-fetched artist could never have imagined that he who creates all existing goods could work without complaint under a system of 'incentive' pay which means that he has to surpass 100 per cent production in order to obtain, for himself and his family, just enough to live, so that he can start the next day all over again. His beliefs too take on a form which corresponds to such production and are put to a use of which he is not informed. Because they, too, are given 'incentives' by appropriate moral rules, and he is forced to compete with his work-mates. But as soon as his productivity has reached a level which assures him acceptable living standards, his output is condemned as too high, and he is sanctioned, in the following way: the production level which he has just achieved, although condemned, is nonetheless recorded. Henceforth, he must reach that same output for less pay, which proves in turn to be insufficient for his daily needs. To cap it all – Sisyphus could have learned a thing or two from them – the door of 'incentive' wages is again thrown wide open, revealing its infinite horizons, and on again goes the record of moral incentives, everything begins and nothing finishes.

There is no way out of this. To make our living, we are forced to provide the rate-fixers with irrefutable arguments for the revision of the norms, and so for the reduction to an ever more unreal level of the time per piece and consequently the pay per piece. This incites us to speed up the rate still more to try and reach a greater level of production. Therefore we prepare the ground, slowly but surely, for yet another increase of the norms.

The cunning threat of the production graph contains this inescapable trap. There is only one thing to do: forget it. But for how long? Doesn't the very first production meeting of the year anticipate the exact extent to which it will be possible for us to forget the chains that we have wound around our own bodies?

After an interminable litany of production data, the foreman pauses a second and then says, in a solemn voice, 'During the first quarter of this year, the level of production in this section exceeded 130 per cent, just as it did in the final quarter of last year. You will therefore understand, comrades, that the current norms are out of date. Believe me, the officials who fix the norms are very patient. Management believes that a general revision is long overdue. The section held its own very well during the rat-race at the end of the year, and it was only because of this that I was able to use my weight to prevent any revision until today.'

Most of us are smoking cigarettes with heads lowered, or staring through the window at the factory yard, which never seems to alter. Everyone remembers that at the last production conference, the chief foreman said: 'Management counts on all turners, and more especially on this section, to do everything possible to end the year on a successful note. The government's economic commission has set us the task of ironing out this factory's main difficulties during the course of the coming year. It is in the interests of everyone that, by pulling our weight, we get on top of the situation into which the factory has fallen through no one's fault. I need scarcely add that we are in duty bound by the trust which the superior authorities have placed in us.'

We knew what he meant all too well. Our factory's products proved unsellable. In the fifties, they had benefited from the prestige attached to the mechanization of agriculture and were therefore subsidized. It had now become essential to turn round the factory's whole production programme in the shortest possible time. This transformation began during the sixties, but the introduction of the economic reforms made it a matter of urgency: the government gave us an ultimatum.

Many left. Many new workers came, mostly from the country – to them the wages were all that mattered. But quite a few of the older workers, precisely those who should have foreseen that a massive revision of the norms would be the climax of this change-over, and who should have put the others on their guard, for example by slowing the rate of work or threatening mass resignations, were the very ones who gave in to this sentimental appeal. They reckoned that they could loot unpunished: after all, they were no longer doing this only for themselves, but because they had been asked to play their part in the great transformation.

It would be an exaggeration to maintain – although the factory journal naturally did so – that these workers, who already knew from past experience what kind of thanks to expect, speeded up their work out of 'love for the factory' or through 'pride in labour'. It would be more accurate to speak of a blind and desperate faith in justice, of the belief that perhaps, after all, this exceptional situation would lead to a truly exceptional transformation. If the management asserted that, in the final analysis, only the workers could save them from the sufferings of a pitiless reorganization, surely this time management would grant the workers some recognition for their efforts?

I watch the workers' reactions. When it becomes clear in the production meeting that all their hopes have been in vain, they do not give way to anger but begin to console themselves: the money we made in the rush at the end of the year is ours, and they can't claim that back from us. Anyway, the justice we had longed for would not have meant more than this: the revision of the norms would not have taken place at once, but would have been postponed for, say, a year. Clearly, in their heart of hearts the workers never believed in their hopes for a second. This was why their hope could change so fast into the hopeless but bearable certainty that tomorrow is another day, and that they will manage somehow.

Has something changed? No one can admit to himself any more that for months he had believed things might change and that he had also worked for such a change. Football, beer, motor cycles, the house and TV programmes regain their rightful places. Other subjects, such as they are, merit at most a few words now and then – but aren't worth an argument.

EVERYONE is on his own. Alone he pursues a daily battle against machines and time. Defeat cannot be shared: how could we want a common success? The worker on piece-rates is accountable only to himself, for his successes or failures. How can he make his mate answer for something which is his own responsibility, when he exceeds the norms and hastens their readjustment? Even if his mate agreed to renounce the perilous pleasures of looting, the two of them would have no influence over the rest of the workshop, 'Good' jobs are scarce, and the foreman decides who gets them. The slightest suspicion of a secret understanding between two individuals, and his disapproval would at once be reflected in their pay packets.

The foreman has absolute right to divide up the work as he sees fit. Very few jobs have to be done on a specific machine. Such work is paid by the hour, and those who carry it out gaze upon the common herd of piece-rate workers with a cool, comprehending air of detachment. Hourly workers, however, have no reason to feel superior: the time-keepers are already swarming round their machines working out how to put them on piece-rates. The foreman reminds them often enough that they owe their status as hourly wage workers entirely to him, that the rate-fixers fight hard to get them put on piece-rates, and that if he, as foreman, is not able to show good results, he will not be able to defend them much longer.

Every pair of milling machines is more or less the same, consisting of a horizontal and a vertical milling machine. The lathes, too, are almost all of the same type. Despite this nothing unites us: we are so divided that we do not even notice the artificiality of being split up into brigades.

Almost everyone in the section is a member of a brigade. After two months, I learned that I had been attached to the

'First of May' brigade; to this day, I have no idea who the other members are. Twice a year, usually on a feast day, the foreman calls us into his office to let us know whether we have won the right to a special bonus, the title of 'Socialist Brigade', or a new voluntary contract.

The foreman decides who belongs to which brigade, and the trade union secretary lets us know the decision during a meeting. His last speech seems to have been typed up in several copies, because I can quote what he said to us from a yellowing copy which I found inside the brigade's ledger – which is carefully preserved in the foreman's office: 'Our basic idea is that the brigades should reflect the complex character of the workshop.'

That is to say, a brigade is not composed of workers involved with a single type of machine, but includes an assortment of borers, millers and turners. This most effectively prevents members of a brigade from discussing anything in common, or from regulating the level of production to defend themselves against revisions of the norm – even if this were possible.

Furthermore, this division into brigades excludes all possibility of cooperation in production. It even prevents rivalry, if that has anything more to it than this bitter struggle against ourselves and against others which goes on quite independently of the brigades. Piece-rate work is, in itself, a source of rivalry, and it makes little difference whether they call it that, or not, whether they get your agreement to it, or not. We surrender to it completely on our own account, and sometimes we may learn that our brigade has benefited.

The competitions between the brigades don't stir much water. 'They've also got to have their little pastimes,' said somebody. He treated the game with understanding, recognizing that it was management's attempt to stick on to our struggle for survival the emblem of a disinterested morality and class consciousness.

It is a bit like the luck of the draw: a few days before the brigade totals are announced, we amuse ourselves by making little bets. Our guesses are usually pretty similar and close to

the mark, since the brigades follow each other at the head
of the table with a striking regularity.

The head foreman takes his duty very seriously. He likes
to talk about 'responsible decisions', arising from 'the
barometers of production'. Almost every time, he explains
that the rules have been rather too liberal, but that from
now on the assessment of the brigades will be much more
severe, and the awards will have to be thoroughly deserved.

Once a year, about Christmas time, they distribute
bonuses to those decorated with the title 'Socialist Brigade'.
But the amount of money involved is none too high.
(About 200 or 300 forints a head; an individual could get
up to 500.) However little it is, it remains welcome. There
are always those who feel they've been sold short, even
though the foreman makes a point of saying that the sum
at his disposal was not sufficient for him to give a hand-out
to everybody who 'deserved' it.

One who did get a bonus justified his delight with an
interesting argument. The following Monday, in the showers, he was nettled by the others: had he been able to tuck
some under his belt, or had his wife taken the lot? According
to him, the brigade contest was the invention of a decent
chap. He thought that upstairs, at least, someone didn't
want the factory to grab everything, and he had invented
the bonus system so that the worker gets something back
from what he produces. No one contradicted him.

But someone else in the changing room may have got
closer to the truth, commenting on an article in the morning
paper. 'Mark my words. They're never going to leave us in
peace with their brigade contests, which they'll change
completely. They are pushing the economic managers
to really get on to them. My brother-in-law works at X,
on an agreed hourly wage. Over there, they have a clever
little scheme whereby they pay bonuses only for over 100
per cent output in the competition results; which is another
way of saying that the race is the only way to get a decent
wage. They have dragged the production graph upwards
through rivalry. They'll do the same everywhere, you wait
and see.'

In this factory that's still a secret of the future. For the time being, payment by results is enough to ensure rivalry. But competition, in one form or another, is part of our lives. It follows us into our homes, and makes us its slaves. Look at the main interest of the majority: football, a competitive sport. Only rarely, perhaps when a sportsman falters, does it cross our minds that we finance this planned world of artificial competition, and that we keep it going in ways of which we are unaware. By identifying with a particular team each of us trains himself for competition. We believe the press and television when they incessantly plug the idea that competition – within sport and outside it – is itself a magnificent aim of life, and that the victorious are a marvellous breed. Factory slang is dominated by the language of competitive sport: 'to deliver a K.O.', 'to run into the ground', and so on. In short, we accept the fact of competition and its spirit, and so cannot even pose the question of whether it could be replaced by cooperation in life and in work, or why competition has come to dominate our conditions of life.

Nothing can stop the factory newssheet – in its clumsy jargon of enthusiasm – from calling an increase in productivity 'the victorious achievement of output totals', as if this was a triumph of officially sponsored labour competition. (It does not include revisions of the norm among the other competition results.) Such articles – the habitual sideshows of competition – along with photographs of the winners, and so on, get a cold reception from those who bother to read them at all. 'Clowning' they call it, even when it's their turn to be among the victorious, or when they have to play the rules of the game and make a commendation to the editor of the brigade journal. They gladly leave all that to the good boys who want a political future and are laying the basis of a career.

It isn't that such tasks require any great effort. The cliches necessary to formulate resolutions stripped of all meaning have been around for a long time; and those to whom 120 per cent means a minimum – for reasons unconnected with morality – are certainly capable of carrying out ceremonial duties. But the situation is an embarrassing one: everyone is aware of the ridiculous and undignified role he plays in this charade; its seriousness is ensured by the foreman, silent and attentive, but always very much in evidence. Everyone knows that before the brigade meeting he and his cronies have already decided on the commendations, and no one mistakes the meaning of his silence.

THEY, THEM, THEIRS: I don't believe that anyone who has ever worked in a factory, or even had a relatively superficial discussion with workers, can be in any doubt about what these words mean. In every place of work, without any definitions or specification, without any gestures, special tones of voice, winks of the eye or a pointing of the finger, *them* means the same thing: the management, those who give the orders and take the decisions, employ labour and pay wages, the men and their agents who are in charge – who remain inaccessible even when they cross our field of vision. The word lumps together those whom one knows and those whom one does not know, those whom one likes and those whom one hates, the foreman with whom one is on friendly terms, the design engineer whom one addresses formally, the manager whom one approaches with obsequious respect, the secretaries, the time-keepers, the inspectors, the factory journal and the guards. Although we mainly talk about factory matters, *them* transcends the walls of the factory, and encompasses – quite unemotionally – everything which is above, far away, outside the power of whoever is speaking. *Them* are all those upon whom he depends in an elusive and indefinable way: those from whom he receives this or that; by whom he is ordered about; or those who are simply strangers – officials from organizations, politicians, television producers, doctors, policemen, or officials at the football ground.

This *them* is both simple and complex, but there is never any doubt about what is meant by it. In conversation it does not give rise to confusion or ambiguity. The most disturbing thing is the complete confidence and naturalness with which the expression is used, without the least emphasis, exactly as one might say, 'my wife', 'my job', or 'let's go round to my place'.

I have also worked in offices in which, just like here, they had directors and subordinates, some of whom were privileged and others on low salaries, big fat vegetables and busy little squirrels. But nowhere, except among factory workers, have I heard this absolute *them*, peremptory, exact, and crystal clear. This usage not only differentiates industrial workers from others; even within the factory it traces a subtle demarcation line between the majority and those whose posts or qualifications are such that they lose sight of the distance which divides the common destiny: dropping *them* is the first sign that someone really wants to start climbing the ladder.

It is an astonishing enigma, worthy of the pen of a linguist or a philosopher, that in contrast to this *them*, through which the workers define themselves by exclusion, workers never use, either by chance, or in jest, or by slip of the tongue, or in error, and probably not even in their dreams, the *us* which forms the counter-balance to it.

The factory journal, and the management from top to bottom, do it all the time. They are always using *us, we, ours* and *with us*. Maybe this *us* is the first word which a freshly promoted boss has to learn; and learn in its full meaning too, because its sense is in no way identical to the spoken word of common language.

In the factory, *we* is used in a way curiously at odds with its dictionary meaning. This little word, which brings to mind the idea of community and togetherness, acquires in the bosses' mouths shades of warning and a mark of distinction which separates them from the rest. Perhaps just because we know who is talking? Because it's not the first time that we've seen him? He says *we*. 'We have made it our aim ... our objective is', or '... we decided ... we achieved ...' You can feel in his words that he wants you to know his part in fixing the aim, as much as the aim itself; that he speaks of *our* objective not only to stir up enthusiasm, but also as a warning: he will be making the reckonings. The word implies unity, in making decisions and implementing them, but when he uses it, it does not mean that this unity really exists, but rather that it is deposited in him alone.

This use of *we* has its own force and direction; which comes from above and radiates outwards from a single point. As soon as that direction is reversed it shrivels away.

'*We* absolutely must finish the component replacement assignment in this coming month. It is urgent,' one of the directors of technical services states during a production meeting. 'That can't be done,' says a worker, and he begins to explain why. '*We* will look into the problem,' replies the director, as unaware as anyone else that his *we* does not mean the same thing in his two statements. The difference would only strike someone who didn't know how our work is planned. People here don't bother about the difference, because they know without thinking about it that the first of these two *we's* divides itself, every moment of the day.

To protect this *we*, television, radio and press return time and again to debate the question: 'who really is a worker?' No sooner do they take it up than they drop it again. Obviously the purpose of such discussions is to expand the meaning of the word; ideologically they must link hegemony to the workers. The most interesting aspect of these debates is the way in which all the participants never stop reassuring each other they are all workers. Such a magical metamorphosis has some strange effects in certain intellectual circles, for example in schools and colleges, which know of workers only from television and which have convinced themselves that in reality workers do not exist.

Once I saw a lone, real worker taking part in one of these televised debates. Everything he said was desperately clumsy. He came back again and again to the same question. How could someone who is not a worker possibly be a worker? Obviously, he did not have sufficient grasp on the deeper meaning of the discussion ... His haughty adversaries were in no position to reveal their hidden purpose, so they did nothing but torment him: he must prove it, argue to the point, define what he meant! But the worker didn't have any definitions. His opponents constantly referred to novel peculiarities in productive processes, and developed complex political theories. The worker did not contradict any of this, but he clung to his standpoint and kept asking obstinately: how could someone be a worker when they weren't a worker?

He was not in a position to say what he really felt and maybe he would not have known how to say it anyway, even though he knew the novel peculiarities of the productive processes at first hand. Anyway, he would have had to name hard facts which are unspeakable in polite society, now that hegemony has been attached to the working class.

No arguments of this sort take place in the factory. There, everything is straightforward: each is what he is. Such criteria as: What was he before? What was his father? How far does he play a part in production as a worker? are not posed, nor does the question 'Who is what?' arise. The management says *we*, but that doesn't create any ambiguities for anyone, even for management themselves. They are perfectly well aware that this *we* does not mean *us workers*.

There is an ever-increasing number of people in factories who are neither workers nor bosses. But even they do not create any ambiguity, whether you look at them from below or from above. In our day-to-day relations with them, personal impressions are a great deal more reliable than any scientific definitions.

'All, or nearly all those who are not workers ...' Pay attention to this: they are non-workers. All or nearly all those who in one way or another give orders; implement rules; fix the conditions of work; caution; control and share in the power of the bosses, even if the individuals concerned have no power in their own right. They constitute the company, not us, and the company is a power over us. They concern themselves with us, while we ourselves are concerned with materials, machines – and above all, with our pay. We work only in the Factory; they work for the Company. They themselves do not decide what their function is, but it amounts to this: registering us, organizing us, protecting us, classifying us, insuring us, keeping us together, keeping us apart, managing us, measuring us, paying us, hiring us, rubber-stamping us, instructing us, sanctioning us, blaming us, decorating us, immortalizing us, silencing us, deputizing for us, observing us, examining us, surveilling us, searching us.

Even if all of this is not clear to him, every worker is familiar with the tone of voice in which the content of power relates to real power in the way that temporary immunity from a weak vaccination compares to perfect health.

The clerk who works in the foreman's office doesn't earn a lot of money, because she is a clerk, and because she is a woman. But she can send for me, pass on orders from the chief, do me favours, or discriminate against me. It is unthinkable that a wages clerk should ever ask me what time would be suitable for me to come along and sort out a problem in calculating my pay. He or she tells me when I must come, and sends me away again if it turns out to be a bad moment for him or her. The records clerk, that rat swathed in red tape, can bang his window down on my nose; the security guard can order me with a glance to stand on one side; the factory journalist may interview me, with my foreman's agreement, and it is the foreman who tells me what I must say.

The official type may be a busy body—he may be devious, cold, double-dealing, provocative—but his behaviour leaves no doubt that his ridiculous little position is part of the power of the factory, of its power over me. Beyond a certain limit his friendly moods and good humour fade away, simply because he must make his position felt. In the factory, everyone who is not a worker has the institutionalized possibility and opportunity to humiliate the workers – if only with his tone of voice. The opposite is not true.

'We know better than you. Leave it to us, OK?' 'Well now. What's the problem?' 'What a lot of trouble you are!' 'These trousers won't do? How long will you go on fussing?' 'Say, that's a pretty work-sheet for you!' 'Can't you learn to fill in a form? Make an effort, use your head.'

A share in the power of the factory sometimes means little more than having this chance to humiliate others, and so it is used at every opportunity. It is cushioned a bit only by the hierarchy of the shop floor. The farther one descends, from experienced skilled workers (provided they are not too old) and those with key positions, down towards the unskilled apprentice, the more these miserable shadows of power approach their true ideal: the sergeant major. Labourers at the bottom of the ladder put up with a pressure which is sometimes unbearable.

One day a young gypsy labourer, said to be a bit crazy, and in a way the section's jester, was suddenly rumoured, to everybody's astonishment, to have applied for Party membership. Mocked about this in the morning break, he retorted: 'I'm going to become a comrade, and that bitch can lick my arse.' (He was referring to the nice dispatch girl, who, when it came to him, gave free rein to her tyrannical inclinations.) His listeners found this argument completely logical: the coarse formula contained an everyday truth. Only one man made a sarcastic comment: 'Just tell them that at the Party meeting . . .'

Workers realize that petty officials are also subordinates. (After all, they stress it enough themselves when they are looking for an excuse to carry out some particularly unpleasant task.) They, too, live in an atmosphere of dependence and humiliation. Workers don't have to be great psychologists to realize that the attitude of these functionaries towards them reflects what they endure from their superiors. 'It makes him feel better if he can kick me in the arse,' said one after a typical scene when work clothes were distributed. None of this leads to any feeling of solidarity: the piece-rate worker cannot pass insults on to any one else, and suffers enormously when he is kicked around, by those who are not, in principle at any rate, his superiors.

Besides, any hope of solidarity is excluded by the simple, daily experience that white-collar workers do lighter work and accomplish less. Their work is easier and less intense, they don't clock in at the crack of dawn; they don't eat during working hours; and the coffee machines that simmer in their offices symbolize their stake in power, limited though it is.

The fatigue and nervous tension that come from working

on machines under the pressure of the norms make workers constantly aware of the difference between what is demanded of them, and whaf is asked of clerks. An image of the ideal worker, 'disciplined, conscientious, dedicated to work throughout his service', is disseminated by television, radio, and the newspapers as a contrast to their caricature of a loafer. It leaves real workers cold. Nonetheless, when a television programme purported to 'expose' the workers of the capital by showing that at around quarter to two (that is, quarter of an hour before the end of the first eight-hour shift) the consumption of industrial electricity dropped dramatically, while the demand for hot water rose suddenly, they all got very agitated, as if they had been personally insulted, and they made pointed comments about clerical workers.

The factory journal devotes reams of moralizing statistics to the way in which workers squander their time. Who in turn asks how time is used in the offices where such figures are cooked up, and such articles written? A clerk who never thinks twice about making a piece-rate worker wait, although the latter is engaged in an incessant battle against time, can make what explanations he likes. He will not be believed. For a worker on production, with his relentless time-table, the office clerk is the personification of a parasite.

How directors use their time, and the intensity of their work, is never raised – there are no criteria appropriate to this world of representatives and conferences. The unaccountable character of such activities makes notions like 'loafing' or 'keenness' pointless: if they were not meant to be bosses, then they would not be where they are. The work of subordinates can be measured and assessed. Bosses, however, have the independence of judges: the good boss has his staff firmly in hand, and drives them as hard as they will go. Of course, the harsher subordinates are treated, the more they reproduce this severity, never missing the slightest opportunity to make us feel their tiny part in the responsibility and power of the factory. So all the greater is our satisfaction when a boss upbraids a subordinate, for we want to see our work become freer and easier. But this hope is doomed, given the way things are: we piece-rate workers, we are the ones who are severe on ourselves.

The only satisfaction the piece-rate worker has is the belief that ultimately he is going to squeeze good money out of the company. He must believe this, as some compensation for everything else. When office staff, who may not even earn as much as he does, come and tell him off in front of others, he soon loses his sense of balance. He has to take these rebukes personally, and when he gets home, irritable and exhausted, he finds a way of scoring off these injuries in his imagination. Even so, he has enough experience to know that ultimately it's not the staff but he himself who is asking for trouble.

Those who have regular contact with the administration hate exaggerated good manners as much as dry, neutral and coldly impersonal behaviour. Maybe workers are wounded when it becomes manifest that they are *pieces*, just as the job they handle is a *piece* in *their* hands. Politeness coming from an administrator is identical to my own complete lack of feeling when faced with a job I am about to mill; it is just part of his technical know-how. The most tolerable petty administrator is one who is jocular, mildly collusive, almost paternalist, even if you have heard his hackneyed patter a thousand times before. The workers expect him to put on a bit of a show as he does his duty to the company.

When the clerk is a woman, we expect her to pretend to flirt with us, as if the matter itself was incidental; when he is a man, we expect him to exchange a few words about some trivia not connected with the factory – male complicity is better than nothing. We don't mind if the same phrases are trotted out from one end of the year to the other.

Tension is a lot more frequent in dealings with powerless subordinates than with the real directors. Few things that come from them cause any offence: our relations with them are utterly without ambiguity, our dependence on them is overt and self-explanatory. The bosses don't need humiliation to enforce submission – they have that in advance.

One rarely hears the director's right to exist or his function and necessity called into question. The reverse is true in relation to office staff and inspectors. Workers have no idea about the world of the bosses, much as the fish of the sea depths know only those predatory species which sometimes penetrate among them, while the surfaces of the oceans, fresh air, land, and mountains are no more than fiction and myths. They apply the notion of the superfluous – a shadowy notion anyway, which can take on weird forms – only to that bit of the world they experience.

MY ME ÓS* – the inspector responsible for my row of machines – introduced himself with these words: 'I hope we're going to get along. I'm popular with the guys here.' He looked around obviously expecting the worker who was training me to confirm this.

'The old fellow does go on a bit, but he'll stamp your pieces without too much fuss,' my instructor said as the inspector moved on. 'His special stunt is never to give his approval to a series straightaway. You show him your first piece and he always asks you to tinker with the settings a bit. But don't bother to change a thing. Get the run going, and next time he comes your way, show him another piece. More often than not, he'll stamp your work-sheet at once, because he's ashamed. He knows very well you can set the machine, but he must try and prove his worth.'

Our inspector is a gentle soul, an elderly man with greying hair and rosy cheeks. He has a childlike affection for his personal vernier. ('Nobody pays me extra to use my own.') The only thing is, he loves to gossip. He has developed a peculiar technique of conversation in order to reconcile his urge to communicate with the workers' reticence. (This resistance is not personal. So long as he doesn't pester them unduly with his inspection, he can do what he likes. If the workers don't like him hanging about their machines, it's because we have no topic of conversation in common with him, and it interferes with our work. But we can't send him away, because he has means of getting his own back.)

He talks in a monologue without expecting any response. He tells endless stories about his time as a soldier, and about the war when he was a lieutenant and got entangled in all sorts of disputes with his superior officers. His stories repeat

*Agent of the M. E. O. (Müszaki Ellenörzö Osztály), or technical control section.

themselves regularly but he always manages to embellish them with new arguments to prove some point long buried in the past.

He is so obviously superfluous that he makes a theme out of it, and weaves it cleverly into one of his war tales, which he tells in the form of a parable: the soldiers would not stand the daily ritual of inspections, but suddenly something made them realize that there was a good reason behind every rule.

One of our turners couldn't stomach having the old man hanging around him. The story goes that one day he told him that since he was standing around with bugger all to do, he might as well hand across the pieces while continuing to blabber on. Since then our *meós* confines himself to inspecting this turner's work. He checks every measurement of each piece three or four times before passing it. He wants to prove that cheek gets you nowhere and that if you don't lose time one way, you lose it another.

The other inspectors are much less ill at ease about their manifest inactivity. They have a few little tricks up their sleeves, and no one expects more from them. They are past masters of false bonhomie, which neatly encapsulates their own idleness and our hard work. Together this self-irony and the jokes about giving every man his due exactly express that condescending benevolence which goes with being an inspector. 'Well then, let's go and see what our bread-winner's been up to!' 'There's no need to look like an orphan. I'll be along to see you.' 'All right, all right, I'm coming. I can see you have a real craving for work!' 'So you've got going already.' 'You're really cracking along there, are you saving up to buy a car?' 'Now all she needs is a little smack on the back-side to make her run,' etc., etc.

You very rarely find them seated at their little tables, installed between the rows of machines. If they stayed there all day long, waiting for us to call them, they would be on hand when they were needed – as our *meós* is. He stays put beside the machines. But the others prefer to loiter in the chief inspector's room or chat in the foreman's office. We always have to go and find them, and then they act as if they are busy men in a hurry to get back to work.

The *meós* are famous for their appetites, but I think that this is a talent of circumstance: eating makes it easier to kill time. There's a small stove in the control room where they cook eggs, sausages, and peppers. They bring along the necessary from home. The workers have only one chance to eat – during the twenty minutes' morning break – and they take a pretty dim view of all this culinary activity going on under their noses. Pavlov's dogs! The stench of machine oil and burning metal mixing with the aroma of fried onions doesn't tickle the appetite; it does make you want to vomit and stirs up feelings of hatred.

A young apprentice regularly provokes rows with one of the *meós*: during the morning break, when the *meós* is usually absent the apprentice eats at his table without asking permission. The workers find it hilarious if the inspector discovers the youngster and flies into a rage. This happens time and time again. I don't think it is out of a special hatred for this inspector (the two never have any dealings with each other), rather he enjoys the repeated sympathy of the workers. They generally eat standing beside their tool cupboards: some sit on their boxes and eat off their laps. There are neither tables nor chairs in the crowded workshop – let alone a canteen. But that hardly bothers us: eating and piece-rates are enemies.

One day, our *meós* explained his role to me. 'You're a man of quantity,' he said, standing beside my platform, 'and I'm a man of quality. You're only interested in your pay. You live for the number of pieces. I am paid by the hour precisely because quality is my responsibility. Please don't take it as an insult, but if it was up to you there'd be as many rejects as anything else. Do you know about law courts? Members of the juries are independent not only of the accused, but also of the judge. Well, here, we inspectors play the part of the jury. I examine the pieces that you make, and I declare them to be good or bad. Not even the foreman can give me orders. We are, if you like, a virtually independent section within the factory. The foreman is a judge. He decides how much you will be paid for the pieces. To some extent we also control the foreman. I'm naming no names, but at least once a foreman here waived the penalty for rejects in case he put his own bonus at risk.'

Basically, he is right. But only his bad conscience makes him blurt out that he is the man of quality. Such quality as is produced is produced by me. His only function is to force it out of me. He is the embodiment of the external compulsion which weighs down on me, and it is I who provide the wages which are handed over to him, solely in order that what I produce will at least be usable. Perhaps that does amount to saying that he is the man of quality, but all this really means is that he doesn't force me to produce in quantity. That is done by other means.

A skilled old worker once said to me. 'Inspectors would be redundant if we weren't all forced to loot for a living.' I thought he was trying to say that the uselessness of the inspectors was only apparent. If someone abolished the *meós* without making any other changes we would go wild, and not give a damn about quality. The *meós's* idleness is only evidence of the fact that we have become accustomed to the constraint expressed in their function and that we anticipate it voluntarily, despite our own interests. But that skilled old worker was also thinking about another kind of uselessness: he linked the need for *meós* with the system of wages. He would like to be a man of quality without inspectors. He would like to be a man of quality *himself*.

An inspector compels a certain level of quality from us, but he is nothing but a hindrance from the point of view of quantity. Even if he wanted to, he could not inspect our work without holding us up. He regards his rubber-stamping as a ceremony, and indeed it is equivalent to a benediction which he bestows on me and without which I can't go forward at all. He finds it quite natural that I should have to search him out if I need him. As for helping us, taking part in the work, even if only shifting some materials, that is quite out of the question, even though he has time on his hands.

'This sort of guy drives you crazy,' said my neighbour the turner. 'He could at least occasionally lend a hand to help us fatten him.'

But even if the *meós* were falling over themselves to help us, the bosses would stop them. They are very jealous of their inspectors' reputations and they think that their jobs should be enviable and respected. It's no contradiction that these independent members of the 'jury' have posts on their side, in the union or the Party. Promotion to *meós* should be counted as one of those privileges which can be bestowed on a worker, just as footballers and other sportsmen are often raised up to the level of 'men of quality'.

Since promotion to inspector status is not beyond our reach, it is surrounded by tangles of suspicion, gossip and innuendo. Everywhere, our factory included, you find pretty women who are *meós*, and each worker has his explanation – not necessarily false – of how they got there. A worker repairs the foreman's car without charge which is why, says another, his wife is an inspector in a different section, even though she hasn't got the qualifications needed. But the ins and outs of how an individual becomes a manager is seldom described so profanely: it is invariably surrounded by an aura of sanctity.

So long as they are prepared to drive themselves mad with overwork, most piece-rate workers can equal an inspector's pay. There is therefore also irony and condescension in their attitude towards the *meós*. The crumbs of power, they imply, are not a good substitute for health and youth, which is to say, the ability to endure labour. The *meós* are often sick men, invalids, or ageing workers. But this solicitude comes to an abrupt end, and the relations between workers and inspectors become crystal clear over issues like overtime.

Since the inspectors are on fixed hour wages, a great abyss separates their hours on overtime from those of the piece-rate workers. The *meós* produce nothing: absolutely nothing. They are quite happy to remain like statues on a pedestal; they are content to stand on their function and watch over what I am doing. However, their presence is mandatory, while we do overtime as if it were a treat rather than, for the majority of piece-workers, a necessity to balance the family budgets; or as if the foreman himself was not really expecting us to insist on putting in extra hours. When we do four hours' overtime, we get a bonus of one quarter of the nominal hourly wage for the first two hours, and a half for the third and fourth. It adds up to no more than a few forints. And so it isn't for this petty cash that, after eight hours' solid work, we choose to do another four: we are after the piece-rate, which remains unchanged. Our exhaustion mounts with every fillér earned.

During the night, much of the immense factory hall is shrouded in shadows and at most a dozen machines are still humming. That we are there, working away, has all the absurdity of a dream. Certainly the stroller who is bored out of his mind does not feel relaxed either: but that's not enough to erase the difference which divides us. With the service foreman snoring away in his office, it is the inspector who, in such moments, personifies everything that oppresses us. During these long night hours it becomes possible for the factory to be *conceived* for what it is: in each section between 100 and 120 workers are toiling away; the inspectors are having a bite to eat; a handful of bosses scurry around in the offices; and, at the gate, several security officers sit sleeping, their hands resting on their knees. What can possibly hold such an absurd system together? That is the question I ask myself as my hands work on.

ON THE FOREMEN I heard two interesting opinions, in my training month. Later I was to come across the first again, in all sorts of different guises, but the second turned out to be just a fleeting idea. I only ever heard it once.

'They are emperors here. They hold us all in their hands. They dole out favours as they feel like it. They know all the machines, and if they don't like you they can take the skin off your back. Even while doing so, they'll squeeze all the pieces they want out of you. They know what they're up to.'

This sort of 'technical' appreciation was apparently contradicted by the second opinion which I heard. In a burst of rage, a young worker who turned a semi-automatic lathe said to me: 'That lot, what they do, I mean what they *really* do, could be done just as well by an unskilled labourer, all on his own, if he worked on an automatic machine, and if someone taught him to count. Well, he wouldn't even have to count. Every morning he could distribute the jobs fairly, working from the list of runs, and take them to the machines. If any hitch cropped up, it could be talked over then and there.' I noticed he shrank back, as if he was terrified by the power of his own imagination: his suggestion contradicted the reality of the game we were playing in every possible way. Pushing through his scanty words was the concentrated expression of a world that was upright and collective.

I could see he was furious. No doubt, he had had some sort of quarrel with one of the foremen. But his anger led him a huge step forward: he characterized the greater part of the function and power of our immediate daily superiors as superfluous.

The foreman doesn't just organize our work: first and foremost he organizes *us*. The foremen fix our pay, our jobs, our overtime, our bonuses, and the deductions for excessive rejects. They decide when we go on holiday; write character reports on us for any arm of the state which requests them; pass on assessments of those who apply for further training or request a passport; they supervise trade union activities in the section; they hire, fire, arrange transfers, grant leave, impose fines, give bonuses. Their signatures are essential to authorize any kind of departure from routine. Only information coming from them can be taken as official. They alone have the right to call a meeting.

'It is forbidden to enter the changing-room during work hours without the foreman's permission,' it states, in one-foot-high red letters on the grey changing-room wall. When I first saw this, I immediately thought of the gym masters in my dismal childhood. Are we just a herd of beasts which must be kept within enclosures?

Those who thought up this rule (and who really knows that?) must believe that, without it, the workers would be dashing into the changing-room without the slightest need to do so. The foreman is the one who is allowed to judge which of my needs are legitimate and which are not. His authority derives from such prohibitions. Which is why, in addition, he prevents all 'unnecessary' *individual* disruption of work. For example, in summer a worker may want to take a shower during working hours – a perfectly reasonable thing to do when one is sweating it out at 40 degrees centigrade, in stinking clothes, dripping with perspiration, with hands so clammy that they slide off the levers. Refusal is justified with these words: 'If I let you take the shower, I would have to let everyone do so just when they felt like it.'

In a more remote section of the factory, there is still a foreman who was once a worker and who announced his promotion to his sometime work-mates at an *ad hoc* meeting, telling them, 'Folks, in this life, there's two things you can't choose. Your mother and your boss!'

This story was told to me with great indignation. But it would be wrong to think the disgust was provoked by either the foreman's promotion or his frankness. After he'd related it, the young mechanic who repaired the switch-box on my machine muttered, almost in despair, his eyes popping: 'A bastard like this can insult my mother when he feels like it, but I can't smash him in the mouth.' He was convinced that the foreman, who doubtless did not even know of his existence, had insulted his mother. And from who else would he have taken that?

Most of the foremen in our section, too, have been workers once – including one nick-named 'The Accordionist' and also the head foreman. There are still a few who worked side by side with them once; or at least along with the head foreman, who is younger than his deputies; he's no more than 35.

He set out on the Party line and in no time was promoted to an inspector's job. 'Who would have thought that he was such a politician?' my instructor said to me, regretting that he had never got on familiar, personal terms with him. Many of the older workers had done so, and this made quite a bit of difference to them. 'Gyula's all right: he doesn't treat his old mates like dirt,' one of them said. 'He won't stop where he is. His luck is made, it's all been mapped out for him. He'll end up at the top.' Only the older ones called him Gyula: to the others, he was 'Comrade'.

The head foreman knows exactly what he is doing. He looks young, he is small and neat, and he understands how important it is to be well-turned-out, although a silver tooth spoils his smile. His speech is deliberate, and he knows how to change his tone of voice adroitly, flaring up just at the right moment, retaining his reserve when he laughs. His speeches are fluent, cogent and to the point, and he talks without notes. In general meetings and production conferences, he often starts like this: 'Comrades, you are, all of you, regular newspaper readers ...' He doesn't get bogged down too deeply in 'the political situation abroad', or in 'our duty to the nation'. If he makes use of the orthodox rhetoric, it is only to a tolerable extent. He's good at mixing up journalese and millers' slang. In contrast to most of the factory functionaries, he is never 'a bulletin behind the times'; and he has a real flare for weaving the latest expressions of the day into his vocabulary: 'It is in the interest of all of us ...' is his favourite formula.

'The Accordionist' was also a skilled worker – a turner in fact – but that was much longer ago. He's around 45 to 50 years old, with a weak and sickly look about him and a nervous manner. Some say he's called 'The Accordionist' because he plays the accordion; others because he has a way of pulling his shoulders back every two minutes like someone miming an accordion player. He blurts out opinions in a muddled sort of way, jumping from one subject to the next, and demonstrates his superficiality whenever he gives advice – as he is often obliged to retract it a few moments later. But he doesn't make a scene if you ignore what he tells you and work out a more satisfactory solution yourself. Every morning, 'The Accordionist' divides up the work: he is very experienced at this. With the job-dispenser girl at his heels, he hurries along the rows of machines and, after a cursory hand-shake, reels off the numbers of the various batches. While the girl notes them down he gives the unskilled labourers directions for the distribution of materials. He hides the personal politics involved in the distribution of jobs behind a smokescreen of secondary matters such as the state of the machines. If there are objections, he just does not hear them. If he gets cornered, or is caught unawares, he pleads that he has some urgent business to do, and refers the complainer to the head foreman. As he is not ambitious himself, he gets on well with the head foreman, even though the latter, since he graduated from the Party school, has overtaken him in the factory hierarchy.

The other two foremen work only in the mornings, and they alternate with each other. Old Gyuri is popular with everyone, and has a reputation for kindness. He has a thick moustache, and summer and winter he wears the same blue beret. Often, he gets himself into the fork-lift truck and helps to heave deliveries. When he can give permission for something, he does so, and we turn to him far more often than to the others. When he has to refuse, he points towards the office with the expression of an accomplice and says 'unfortunately'.

'Kazmer' has some strange habits. His behaviour is stiff and ritualized. He always wears clean, brown overalls, although even the head foreman dresses in blue. He hates dirtying his hands. He is very formal with everyone. No one has any idea why his nickname is 'Kazmer', but that's what he is called just the same. He came from a technical school. My neighbour says 'he plays at being an engineer'.

The nominal hourly wage for a piece-rate worker is fixed by the head foreman. He set mine just as he set it for the others. No one else has any say in it, not even the union representative. Once the nominal hourly wage has been fixed between a new worker and the head foreman, 'The Accordionist' uses it as a directive which stipulates the category of job he should hand out. Jobs in a higher category mean higher wages per minute and therefore a better piece-rate, and they go mostly to those with a higher nominal wage. So everyone earns more than his nominal wage, but not a lot more. The extra, of course, comes from looting.

So everyone is dependent personally on the head foreman who fixes the level of his pay: this is a paradox of piece-rates. The only concern one worker has for the others is jealous suspicion. Are the others a few fillérs ahead? Is their hourly rate going up more quickly? Are they getting more of the best 'good' jobs that are going? Such rivalry is equally fierce over all matters in which the head foreman's decision is final: holidays, overtime, bonuses, awards.

Everyone knows that the foremen are swayed by favouritism; indeed they think there's more to it than there really is. The truth is that only a foreman knows how to steer his way between jealousies, grievances, vanities, accusations, resentments and foul tempers inflamed by alcohol. He 'solves' the problems which crop up – caused basically by everyone's forced dependence upon him – with an expression of concern and sympathy and, as the case might be, with jocular or pacifying words.

The scale of hourly rates is from 8 to 12 forints. You

progress along it little by little. Only very occasionally might you get more than two increases in two years. The tension never stops – and it doesn't do anyone any good.

During the personal 'conversations' which precede an individual rate increase, the head foreman rarely refers to matters of ideological principle. In production conferences, however, he never fails to mention 'the struggle against vulgar egalitarianism'.* This 'struggle' never touches on the difference in income between workers and foremen – let alone managers. At least I've never heard anything of the sort. And if the matter were to be fought over, it would not be decided within the factory.

His other pet theory is: 'Comrades will understand that we can distribute only what *we* have produced.' This is clear and exact, and I don't think that anyone could raise the least objection to it. Only the workers perhaps interpret it differently from the foreman. Someone in the row behind me whispers sarcastically, 'He must be going to distribute his own bonus amongst us, since we produced it in the milling department.' Quite obviously the foreman's regal 'we' had left him cold.

It is little wonder that, in individual cases, 'the struggle against vulgar egalitarianism' does not figure in the arguments used. There is not a boss who could explain to a piece-worker why the performance rates are higher or lower from one case to another. Everyone knows perfectly well how they fix the time per piece: then, after this has been established, the job is given a special category; in this way, identical piece-times can mean more money in one case, less in another – and as much extra as each can loot. The foreman divides the work, handing out jobs of higher or lower categories, according to the level of the individual's nominal hourly rate.

The end result is obvious: a young and an old miller are each good for the same amount of work, but their output is controlled in the foreman's office. The 'fight against vulgar

*An ongoing campaign which emphasizes the need for material incentives, and which intensified after the economic reforms of 1968.

egalitarianism' is just a phrase for festive occasions – and even then, it is kept to vague generalizations.

In the individual 'chats' about our wage rates, the foreman turns everything back to personal issues: age, family situation, and the state of the machines. Sometimes, he even goes so far as to say that the norms are chancy and ineffectual; in this way he stresses his independence from the rate-fixers, just as the inspectors stress their independence from the foremen. But this appeal to personal circumstances can sometimes boomerang. Those who suffer these circumstances know them far better than anyone else, and from what they said it often emerged that they would make decisions in a much more human and understanding way – if it was up to them. The foreman's decisions are especially criticized by those not directly involved. The petty advantages which always seem to be given to someone else reinforce the general feeling of competitiveness in everyone.

In principle, the trade-union secretary is supposed to have a say when it comes to revising the hourly wage rates.

With the office of secretary, he does not have to work. He is nominated for the job by the head foreman. To put up or vote for another candidate would be a direct provocation of the head foreman. Anyway, what could possibly come of it? After the election, the head foreman fixes the pay of the secretary, who, in any case, has a second master as well: his superior in the union hierarchy, who works from a desk in the factory office building.

At the moment, our trade-union official is a former turner; his predecessor was one of the inspectors. (The section committee has six members; two are inspectors; one works in the administration.) This turner was a painfully meticulous worker who was never late and did a lot of overtime. He always stopped work half an hour before the siren sounded so that he could clean his machine – which had almost become a part of him. The head foreman said of him – as the highest possible praise – that it had been very hard for him to accept his commission, even though he would not lose financially while he held the position. He too was one of the old guard, on familiar terms with the head foreman. Now he strolls about the workshop aimlessly, or wanders off to visit his friends. When someone comes to him with a problem, he won't discuss it, he just nervously assures him that he will put the matter to the head foreman. The usual result is: 'Its not on, as Gyula explained in the collective meeting, and he's quite right.' The hidden message is that the head foreman dislikes being approached indirectly. If the petitioner persists he eventually gets to the head foreman anyway. But most of us go straight to him in the first place – with a much better chance of success.

The same sort of thing happens over the revision of the hourly wage rates. It is most unlikely that the head foreman has to have an extended argument with the union representative before getting his agreement. But at least the secretary has a knowledge of everyone's personal problems, and his opinion is taken into account.

He has a lot to do only when the brigade conferences come round. He takes part in all of them, usually in the company of one of the foremen. Before the production meetings, he prepares suitable interventions, on the basis of directives given to him by the head foreman. On these occasions, he negotiates with the old guard, while the foreman himself handles the Party members – such as, for example, the young setter. Of course, he also turns up at factory conferences. At *ad hoc* meetings, or production meetings, he reads out a short introduction, or a more developed report, which he might have written himself, but certainly not before consulting with the head foreman.

When he has finished he calls on 'Comrade Gyula D., head foreman', who, for his part, always begins by thanking him for 'his richly informative introduction'.

In principle he cannot intervene in decisions that affect the whole section. They are signed by the factory trade-union representative, alongside the financial directors. The head foreman is told of these decisions first, before the union secretary, but both of them know before we do.

In a way, we don't feel that our union official is really part of a trade-union apparatus at all; we look on him much

more as a straw man, or a string puppet. If he was a career-
ist, we would certainly class him as one of *them*. Everyone
agrees, 'There's only a union because you've got to have a
union. They collect our contributions but when we want
something they spout just like the foreman, "If you produce
more, you'll earn more". The union is our paid enemy.'
'They would be the first to send for the police if there was a
strike.' Enthusiastic press and TV commentaries burst
with solidarity for the union-led wage struggles in the West,
with curious results. Although our trade union is always
credited with 'successes', and – if the factory journal is to be
believed – management can't do a thing without the union's
consent, nonetheless our unions do not seem to compare
favourably. Many (especially the older workers of peasant
origins, but also the youngest ones as well) do not join the
union. When the secretary pressures them gently, they say,
'I haven't got money to throw away for nothing.'

THERE is a collective agreement; almost everyone knows that, but nobody knows what is in it. 'That sort of nonsense has nothing to do with me' is the general opinion. To start with, very few know what is meant by this term 'collective' – that is, the joint elaboration by the factory union and the management of 'mutual rights and obligations'. Those who do know put it rather differently. 'It states everything we have to put up with, except for what it doesn't state', I was informed.

How long is it since the collective agreement was drawn up for this factory? Opinions differ: 'it has always been there', 'it's been around for several years', 'the full details were published for the first time last year', 'last year, they drew up a new one'.

Some could remember that the 'collective' was read out during a production meeting last year. 'But that was only a draft for comment', someone else explained. 'Was there a vote?' They looked at me in amazement. The only one who replied to my naive question said, 'Well, they answered objections – but you can't really object to this sort of thing; then the "collective" was completed, and it was deposited in the office. As for what has been changed since then . . . I just couldn't tell you. I don't pay much attention in production meetings.' During the big rush at the end of the year, I asked for one day's leave. 'I'm not giving days off to anyone; not even unpaid,' said the chief with a shake of his head. I tried to argue with him, but he cut me short. 'Take a look in the "collective", if you don't believe me.' And he left me standing there.

I crossed over to the office and asked the administrative clerk to let me consult the collective agreement. She is in effect secretary to the head foreman. She went to see him, returned and drew out of her desk a thick, photocopied volume. 'If I asked for it you would not give it to me without the chief's consent?' I asked. 'That's the rule,' she replied icily, adding, 'Consult it here. You don't have the right to take it away.'

Within a couple of minutes I regretted not having taken the head foreman at his word. It was simply impossible to find the appropriate clause. There were a dozen entries in the index under the word 'leave', each with long sub-titles, but not one of them seemed to apply to my case.

I asked for help, and the clerk indicated an appropriate heading. I turned to the page and found something like this: 'In accordance with 1972/XIX Min. Tvr. 26 @ (4)-(6), and further in accordance with M. Trvk. 47 @ (5) . . .' (I cannot vouch for the accuracy of the numbers, nor of the abbreviations.)

Once more, I went to the head foreman, and he gave me the following explanation: 'I don't speak hot air. Everything is set out in the regulations. In the "collective", it states clearly that I am not obliged to give you leave.' 'But you could do so if you wished?' 'I could, yes, but it's left to my judgement.' I accepted the inevitable, and since my stubbornness had already lost me twenty minutes I allowed myself another look at this collective agreement.

It consists of some 150 pages, largely covered with tongue-twisting abbreviations, incomprehensible clauses and paragraphs, numbered in a way that's impossible to follow. Even when text emerges out of this jungle, it consists only of a framework of regulations, reiterated in unimaginable bureaucratic–legalistic jargon, as off-putting as possible. Areas of responsibility are very vaguely indicated; lines are drawn sharply only when the interests of the company demand it. Within these limits, it is always left to the relevant chief to decide. A sound principle, because if they had to work according to the agreement they would not be able to take a single step. They know from instinct and experience what the interests of the factory really are, and so never need to enter this maze of regulations. The legal advice columns in the daily papers have an easy job: 'The collective convention of your factory will certainly contain an indication as to the legitimacy or otherwise of the decision against which you are protesting.' That's what they always say in answer to readers who write in with complaints.

My neighbours got wind of my little dispute, and my friend the turner mocked me once again. 'Now you've really shown them, haven't you? Did you expect to find anything in the "collective" which they don't want to have there?' I took a risk and asked him, 'But who are *they*?' 'The union, the company, the whole damn lot.'

M summed up the incident in his own inimitable way: 'Take it easy. They are not going to kick themselves in the ass. Perhaps they are wrong once in a thousand cases – and even then, it's just by chance. The "collective" is for them, and not for you.'

SUPPLEMENTARY WAGES are our most frequent topic of conversation with the foremen. They have at their disposal a relatively large sum for the adjustment of individual wages. No one knows exactly how much, nor whether all or only part of it is used up. The foremen's accounts never mention it, nor can you find any trace of it, under either 'deficits' or 'outgoings', in the official 'bulletin of results'.

Supplementary wages are of great importance to us. Their function – even from the official point of view – is to ameliorate slightly the pay of those who, because of work conditions and through no fault of their own, find themselves short.

The technologists would like us to adapt our movements to the rhythm and power of our machines, to pass the pieces from one hand to the other without any interruption or loss of time, in such a way that we would never deviate from the prescribed motions, even in order to obtain the desired results.

In all this, the greatest obstacle is not ourselves but, so to speak, Nature itself. Maybe one day automation will provide a solution, but, as things are, the factory cannot realize this goal. Its cumbersome organization, and the sheer inertia of our materials, goes against it.

But this shortfall does not operate to our advantage; the factory makes sure of that. Our work is standardized, and the norm rests on the assumption that interruptions do not occur. If I stop when I run into a difficulty, the norm looks on this as a vice rather than a virtue, and punishes me accordingly. It takes a deduction from my pay, as if to force me to offer a sacrifice so as to make amends for not yet being in the paradise of full automatization – in which I will not be needed and where no interruptions will occur.

Supplementary wages are a small correction, like corrections in the newspapers, which always come after the damage has been done, in small print, tucked away at the bottom of the page, and only after repeated protests to the editor – if at all.

Supplementary wages bring the norm down to earth. The norm (whether it is realizable or not) dreams of me as a perfect being made up of a few regulations, who works on immaterial matter, and is interchangeable with any other perfect being without loss of efficiency. The norm recognizes no problem, no chance event, no complication in men or materials. The norm knows men who are ill and healthy men, but it ignores the cough which forces me to put my hand in front of my mouth and which thereby prevents me from raising the piece at the required moment; it ignores sore feet which make me walk slowly; it knows no slackening of concentration, no broken finger-nails, no unpleasant sweating, no satisfaction at having eaten well. It regards machine and materials in the same way. The norm knows good machines and bad ones, but not worn-out levers and gears, spindles out of true, or threadworn screws. It recognizes materials which can be lifted by hand, and others which must be lifted by machine, but not those of an unusual shape, which are difficult to handle, nor those spare parts which are left out in the snow in the factory yard and which still freeze to the fingers when they are brought into the workshop. The norm does not know the malice of swarf which gets into every crevice; or that a new milling head cuts well while the old one cuts badly. It totally ignores the chain of events: a worn-out drill leaves an edge within the hole; you can't put a bolt through it without using force; after twenty pieces, the worker gets tired, slows down, decides not to waste time changing the tool, prefers to suffer from its imperfections, gets even more tired, and so on. External circumstances do not exist for the norm: it knows neither sun nor rain, neither noise nor springtime, neither love nor hate. In fact, the norm knows absolutely nothing; despite this I must do what it says, because if I don't it threatens me with punitive sanctions.

Supplementary wages – a diminutive corrective – cannot be demanded for any kind of difficulty; for them, interruptions of human origin simply don't exist. Supplementary wages take into account only the resistance of machines and materials – and even then within strictly defined limits – for the norm cannot awaken in inanimate matter the will to deny itself, as it can in us.

When, at least in principle, are supplementary wages given?

When materials prove harder than the technical experts imagined, so that several operations are necessary to remove a bed of metal which the blueprint states can be done first time through; this can double or triple the total time for the batch, although pay per piece remains exactly the same, and it's quite impossible to earn a fillér more. Or if the previous operation left a rough edge, so that I have to take it to the polishing machine to smooth it, before I can insert the piece in my own machine. If this happens I must grind the whole batch before I can begin milling. That operation is unpaid. Supplementary wages are intended to compensate for this sort of problem. Batches which have been forged often arrive warped. Those who know about this sort of thing say it is because in the forging-shop hot pieces are thrown on top of each other, and some therefore cool under the weight of others. This means a really hard task for me: I take my six-pound hammer, and try to re-forge the piece when it is stone cold. The grip on the milling machines allows perfect results only when the piece itself is perfect. The margin is about a millimetre. Re-forging is often a complete failure: either the piece won't give at all, or it caves in past the margin at the slightest tap. Fury joins my fatigue as I have to carry out such crude, unpaid work.

Perhaps I would not be able to claim supplementary wages for this beastly hammering if it were not for the fact that it belongs to a category of work for which there is a special rate and a pretty name: 'flattening'. But it works out at very little – 6 or 7 forints an hour. With such jobs, looting is out of the question; it is impossible to finish in the allotted time; and that is often longer than the milling itself.

If a mount breaks and I have to rig up another way of clamping pieces in place, I can ask for a supplementary wage. As I can also if a shortage of tools compels me to do a job 'by hand', or if there is a power cut; but in those cases it has to go on for an appreciable length of time to justify my demand.

In principle, then, all my work is paid for. The system of norms doesn't suffer from any manifest failures, but rather, when coupled with supplementary wages, it reveals itself as perfect and must be applied with ever greater severity – as the constant revision of norms shows. Supplementary wages are an example of fairness, but it is the fairness of the norm itself. They supplement my pay to the level which the norm stipulated it would have reached in the absence of any interruptions. Put another way, my supplementary wages don't supplement my wages one little bit. Rather, they are a part of my pay on which *they* try to economize!

The foremen, setters and inspectors never once mentioned the existence of supplements, and it was only some time after my arrival that I heard about it from old M. 'For stuff this hard you can demand a sweetener,' he said, with a knock on one of the metal pieces. Previously, he had machined this job and he always managed to obtain a supplement for it. But 'The Accordionist' never said a word when he put me on the job.

I spoke to him about it, but I ran into a stone wall of sullen resistance. All the foremen, Gyuri included, do everything to make us feel that supplementary wages are special presents which they hand out to us, for which we give nothing in return. You have to request them, and so, before making even the most legitimate request, I start to suffer from anxiety.

In order to avoid being refused, I tried to get some advice from others. When are supplementary wages considered legitimate? How should one ask for them? The millers are reluctant to answer this sort of question because supplementary wages, too, have come under the spell of competition.

Perhaps it is because no one knows anything precise about them. Only one thing is certain: the foremen resist paying supplementary wages. Each worker therefore con-

cludes that if there are too many demands less will be left
for him. There isn't the slightest evidence to suggest that
this is true – nor that it is false.

So each worker treats what he gets as a supplementary
wage for a particular job almost as a professional secret.
Secretiveness of this sort generates complicity, whether real
or imagined, with the foreman: 'I'll give you a supplement
for this batch – but don't let on to the others.'

Information I got from other millers slipped out unawares in a moment of anger (when they failed to get the
supplement they had asked for) or of delight (when a specific
batch was transformed into a 'good' job thanks to a supplement which was particularly hard to get) or when they protested (because the foreman had neglected to fill in the form
for a promised supplement).

It seemed to me that those of my neighbours who
weren't millers were prepared to talk more freely, perhaps
because of the difference in our respective tasks. For
example, if they discover a tough piece in a batch which
they work before it comes over to me, they take the opportunity of telling me – through the labourer who brings
me the materials – that it would be worth asking for a
supplement. Turners and borers have a reason to persuade
me, the miller, to demand a supplement as well. In this
way, they can avoid the foreman's objection, 'That's
interesting: the miller didn't find anything wrong!'

But everybody reacted alike to my anxiety over how I
should demand a supplement. Suddenly, they were full
of good advice, 'You mustn't give them a moment's peace.
They won't give you a thing. They couldn't ask for anything
better.' 'They know perfectly well what they owe us. They
just play at being little innocents. If it was just up to them
...' (gesture with the fingers). 'The hope is that you'll
simply carry on without complaining, just you tell them
what you'll do if they don't give you a supplement.'

This last piece of advice told me more about the desires
of the man who gave it to me than about reality; he
himself would never follow it. When the foreman digs
in his heels, no one can contradict him. If I don't do the

job because I have been refused a supplement, this constitutes *refusal to work*, which is subject to disciplinary
sanctions.

For example, I receive a run which arrives along with a
supplement form for 'flattening'. But half my time is
wasted in readjusting the pieces, because the pattern I
have to match it with is inadequate. I show it to Kazmer,
and ask him if I can have an additional supplement.
'Let me show you,' he says in a bad temper. He takes up a
hammer; I look at my watch. He bangs away at a piece
for a full three minutes (the time allowed for flattening is
one minute). Then he compares it against the pattern.
It doesn't match. But off he goes, saying, 'Bang away a
little more. It will soon be perfect, they can all be corrected.'
Not a word about a supplement. And I must still think
myself lucky to be getting anything at all for this flattening.

Although supplementary wages complement the norm,
they are not themselves subject to a norm. Reluctantly, the
foreman writes down a rounded-off figure, which is always
less than I expect. 'That is the usual rate for the job,' he
says if I protest.

A rather slow, old worker runs the milling machine
which manufactures nuts. He always does the same job
but the metal is harder than the standard and he is compelled to operate slowly. He doesn't have the strength to
make up lost time by speeding up his own movements.
Several times, he has asked for a supplementary wage -
but always in vain; if the machine runs slower that's no
reason for a supplement. 'They won't even talk about a
supplementary wage if I don't produce at least twice as
much.'

Of course, that isn't to say that for doing double, or
triple, the amount of work we receive proportionate
increases in our supplements. I experience this myself.
I have to suffer a spectacular loss in order to get a fraction
of it reimbursed; otherwise I don't get a fillér.

The time we lose in asking for compensation - often
without success - must itself be counted as an uncompensated loss. If we don't point to the difficulty before

starting, or at the very latest half-way through the run, we have practically no chance of getting a supplement. If the request is made after the job is completed, the foreman just won't believe it – to put it mildly. However, it is only after the run is completed that he will endorse it. First, I have to take my 'money' to the foreman, then to my inspector, and then, when they have finished with it, back to the foreman again. All this takes time and more time.

On top of it all, nothing is easier than to forget to ask for a supplement or to forget to hand in the piece of paper. The boundaries between straightforward 'bad' jobs and those which merit supplements are very fluid. Even if a worker has received a supplement for years for a particular type of job, the day when he forgets to ask for it the foreman won't say a word. Supplementary wages have exactly the same status as normal pay: they are remuneration for work done. Nevertheless, if we don't ask for them we don't get them; if we don't chase after them, we would never see any.

In this way, the foremen economize on wages when these come under their jurisdiction rather than that of the computer. It's improbable that they do this out of sheer laziness. Most workers think that the foremen have a material interest in cutting down supplementary payments to the minimum, although the exact way in which they benefit is not at all clear. Perhaps through bonuses, sharing, or maybe something else. The boldest dare to suggest that they simply put what's left into their pockets.

Someone suggested that at the next production meeting we should ask exactly how much a month was available for supplementary wages. (Prior experience had taught us to ask important questions only when a good number of us had previously agreed to it. When the foreman feels that the questioner is isolated, he doesn't even bother with a subtle reply; if he knows that there's a group waiting to hear what he says, it's not so easy for him to get away with it.) But this proposal did not arouse much enthusiasm. Most of us thought that the foreman would not reply directly, but only through such formulas as, 'that depends on the value of production in the previous months', or, 'much less than I would like to have', or 'the factory's resources are limited'. Someone even suggested, 'He would give you a figure. And then what? How are you going to check whether it's accurate, or whether the whole lot is in fact distributed?' This decided the matter.

We would not ask the question but only after we had considered all possible replies. No one thought it possible that the foreman would be able to say, 'A sufficient amount is available to meet the purpose of supplementary wages, which is to ensure that you never have to do work which is unpaid.'

No one knows if the union has ever concerned itself with the problem of supplementary wages as a whole, or even with individual problems arising out of them.

'You'll be working on two machines at once. What's so surprising about that?' M told me on my first day. I was astonished, and not just because it seemed an amazing idea that I could simultaneously service two of these many-levered, helpless beings which had evidently been designed to depend on one man and to occupy him exclusively. But also because I had no idea that I would suddenly be confronted with two milling machines: none of the many representatives of the administration present at the ritual of my registration, not even the foreman, had thought it significant enough to point this out.

Nor do I believe that they thought I could avoid seeing through the next and even greater surprise, that beautiful box of tricks: piece-rates. Perhaps they just wanted to gain time, because it is only after their probation period that the essence of the two-machine system can be grasped by those who haven't got the faintest clue about it when they begin. But if someone hands in his notice after a few days of the probation period, he still has to work right through it; besides, they never said a word to me about the probation period, anyway.

At the end of my training month, I had learnt enough to begin on two machines by myself; it seemed increasingly unbearable. I persuaded myself that I had seen through the logic which had led to the introduction of this system. I thought, they've noticed all those brief moments when one has a breather, while the machine is fed slowly, the table advances, or when the machine does the milling by itself. But the very fact of being on piece-rates means that I've renounced these or any other breathing spaces.

It is therefore logical that they should also aim to utilize me during these fractions of a minute; for every other possibility had already been accounted for by the special, exhausting 'stimulus' of piece-rates, which only allows money to be earned when the machine is 'alive'. These few moments could be turned to account if, at the same time, I run another series on another machine, prepare a new piece or dismount a finished one. It is immediately apparent that not every job, or every operation, could be run through simultaneously with another. But in the ideal case I could produce twice as much in the same time, and in every instance a great deal more than I could have done with just one machine. With the extra effort the number of pieces increased, and since the piece-rate worker earns his money from exactly this, the system was 'stimulating'.

At this point, it seemed to me that the two-machine system was acceptable. After all, piece-rate workers are not looking for an easy time (even if they really want it, they don't get much choice in the matter). They live from looting, they pledge themselves – with mockery, one might add, of their own free will – to a total mobilization of strength, nerves, and health. From the moment they accept the piece-rate system and the norm, they ought to welcome two machines as an offer of new opportunities: not for *something else*, but to perfect the same. That the factory gets something out of it is quite understandable, for otherwise they would never have introduced it.

That was how I first thought about it; it was simply looting: the pressure of incentives became the reality of my state of mind. It would have been grotesque not having used this possibility; this was a matter of instinct not calculation. The only kind of calculation I could afford – which, in those days, I thought I could afford – was to reckon *how* to use this possibility. I strove to combine my work in such a way that the second machine took up only what would have been my breathing spaces, and to avoid the two series interfering with one another. And so, I worked on the second machine only during my brief moments of dead time on the first, and not throughout all of them, either. This enabled me to maximize my use of one machine. I did not let the situation bother me; it was in my interests; it produced a 'net gain' for me.

The truth was that I still had not got to the bottom

of the system. I began to realize this when I could not detect a significant difference on my pay slip between my total pay on those days when I worked with one machine, and those when I used two. Sometimes the former was better; sometimes the latter. Perhaps the real results would show up clearly on the ten-day bulletin.

But as it happened, I didn't have to wait for that. During an afternoon shift, Kazmer sent two batches over to me. As my shift-mate had left a run of fifty pieces from the morning, I had a choice. I thought over the various combinations, assessed the rhythms of the three different types of work, and decided that it would not pay me to combine two series simultaneously. I got going on one machine, and, during the slack moments, I set the other in a leisurely way so that I would be able to start it immediately after finishing the first batch.

Kazmer watched me for a while at a distance, then he ambled over. 'You're not working the horizontal miller?' I began to explain my calculations, and to assure him that with the setter's help I would almost certainly finish quicker than by trying to mill the two batches at once. But Kazmer's problem was not the same as mine. 'That,' he said, 'is your affair.'

'I am only asking because I see that you have work for the other machine as well,' he carried on as if he had not heard my explanation. 'Your horizontal miller's in working order, isn't it?' I nodded agreement, without understanding what he was getting at. 'Then, I'm only telling you that I can't stamp any of your batches, "for one machine": it's not even worth the bother of asking me.' And, as if to reinforce his argument, he added, 'Have a look. You'll see, your work is all for two machines.'

And so I discovered that the small box in the bottom left-hand corner of my 'money' – in which appeared either the number 1 or 2 – did have a meaning after all. No one had explained what 'T.g.r.: 2' meant. I couldn't really blame my instructor; after all, his job was to teach me milling.

Kazmer's fragmentary explanation was as follows:

'This figure here indicates whether or not you must work on another batch alongside it. If it's marked "2", well, that's it: you must work on two.' It was clear that he already regretted having spoken about this. Through his hesitant words emerged the outline of a supplementary wage previously unknown to me which we could ask for ('in moderation', he said) in cases when work marked 'for two machines' had to be carried out on one, because the other, for reasons beyond the operator's control, was not working, perhaps because it had broken down, or just because there was no suitable batch for it. This type of supplementary pay was called 'marked for one machine'.

Already, experience had taught me that if there was any question of supplementary wages, it meant that somewhere a lot of unpaid work came into it. Why should I be compensated (even 'in moderation') for work I had not done, and which would be paid at the normal rate in any case, when I got around to it? Through sheer generosity?

The answer seemed unbelievable, but soon enough it became an ordinary, self-evident aspect of my daily work. The tag 'for two machines' indicates that the piece-rate is only half the normal pay per piece, calculated by the usual methods. This 'T.g.r.: 2' is no sign of kindness by the rate-fixer, with which they let me know that I can earn a little more on the piece in hand if I choose to run another machine as well. On the contrary, it means that on jobs marked by the rate-fixer's office 'for two machines' (which is about 70 per cent of my work) I'm obliged to work on the other machine as well. I must make two pieces for the pay of one, if I want to avoid getting only half-pay for one piece. This was the end of mathematics – at least for me.

The rate-fixer's office does its work well. It marks 'for two machines' all those jobs when the machine runs on its own, if only for a fraction of a minute, not even enough to take the next piece from the trolley and bring it over. They write 'for one machine' only in cases when it is absolutely impossible even to think about another machine. The work done in the rate-fixer's office is not very complicated: merely a matter of simple division. They divide the time per piece, and the corresponding pay per piece, by two. Their efforts could hardly have been less; all that happened was that they acquired new machines, and created a new heading to go with them.

Our 'money' does not carry the least trace of this division; the piece-time is left just as it normally is. This detail, therefore, has absolutely no relationship to the true time. No doubt, this would seem to be an insolent mockery if we didn't already look on the piece-times as nothing more than a glorification of the rate-fixer's imagination.

In these circumstances it is almost a luxury, a waste of the factory's money, to make use of a multiplying factor for certain types of work. (This is marked on our money as $\times 1.1$, $\times 1.17$. The multiplier never reaches 1.2.) It means that the pay per piece is not exactly half that 'for one machine', but a little bit more, a fifth more at most. This makes hope sparkle again. It holds out a promise: if I work on two machines in the given time, and manage to double my output, not only will I get my basic pay, but I will get a tenth extra for having produced twice as much. This multiplying factor is sheer generosity on the part of the rate-fixers. Division by two would be quite enough, the extra tenth is hardly more of an incentive to work faster on the two machines than a straightforward 'T.g.r.: 2'.

If an expert on norms had secretly watched me when I grasped the nature of the two-machine system, he would have been rubbing his hands with delight: the moment I saw the truth I was transformed into someone for whom work (the more the better) had become a necessity of life. Thanks to the system of norms, piece-workers are already living under communism – at least as regards jobs marked 'T.g.r.: 2'.

This put a stop to my speculations about whether or not to put batches through simultaneously. Whatever came my way, I carried out on two machines. Until then, I thought it a net gain if, while working on one machine, I also did something on the other. That remains true, with the following modification: each piece I manage to make on the other machine helps to diminish my losses. Until then I utilized a possibility; now I am its slave.

I cannot allow myself to put any job on one side. Even if the combination is virtually impossible the foreman just shrugs his shoulders. I have work; both my machines are running; he cannot give me a supplementary wage. If I am stubborn and work only one machine, even for months on end, I hurt no one except myself. If I work on just one machine, in addition to its usual profit, the factory makes on each of my pieces a bonus of half pay per piece, even though I would not be producing less than when the one-machine system was in force.

Working on two machines at once is very difficult: it is dangerous and exhausting; you have to use all the brains you've got. When I work on one machine, it is boring and tiring, certainly, but the moments during which it functions automatically do lead to some satisfaction. It seems that I dominate the machine: I have fed it, my hands rest upon its casing, and now it works. It's true that I only feel these almost tender sentiments when I switch from two machines to one; even then, they vanish after a little while. But when I am working on two machines, such feelings are utterly impossible. You can't dominate two machines: they dominate you. They devour raw materials and vomit them out finished. Full of impatience as if they are jealous of each other, each demands that I immediately complete the work on each of them. There is absolutely no question of even a shadow of relaxation, or a hint of satisfaction, as you dismantle one piece at lightning speed, insert another, unscrew the clamps, screw them up again, and immediately get going on the other machine to do the same thing, but with a different rhythm, and when you've done that, to recommence on the first one, all over again.

I change into a senseless, mindless machine. This shows not so much in the disappearance of every kind of sensation or feeling, or in the fact that ideas flee from me, but above all, in the devastating despair caused by the very awareness of a thought or feeling. They upset me, irritate me, send me into a rage, all but annihilate me. I must fight against thoughts and invent ways of doing so, just as in childhood I had to count to send myself to sleep. The machines themselves help me to find ways to do this. Their different rhythms add up to a new rhythm, which I take up, flow with, and try to anticipate: this almost gives me pleasure, because I feel that I am approved of and confirmed by the machines. To become aware of a thought is as much of a hindrance to my work as a fault in the machine, slippage in a spindle, stiffness in the speed controls, or the jamming of the starting button. In the same way, a clear thought emerging in consciousness is also the enemy of relaxation, of that relaxation close to suspended animation into which you plunge when you get home from work. I react to them with the same hostility as in the factory and with the same wish to flee from them as when I am at work. In such moments, I know that I still belong to the machine, that I have not yet regained myself. But if someone lives like this from his childhood on, does he know that there is anything to regain?

Even at work, when I have found the rhythm and become one with the machine, thoughts and feelings do not disappear: they change. What disappears is the direct relationship which unites them with me, the identity between me and them. This is very difficult to communicate. The best way I can put it is like this: *I* cease to exist. When the huge side-doors of the workshop are opened and the transporters rattle in loaded with material, I *know* – without having a thought as such, I simply *know* – that I am in a freezing draught, but I do not *feel* that I am cold. My back aches, there is cramp in my fingers, the piece-rate is ridiculous: I don't feel or think any of this. I only know that someone who is me feels them and thinks about them, I don't even feel or think about my work itself; I don't organize it; I only register that I am working. I know that it is I who has stopped the machine at the right time, that it is I who bends down to pick up the next piece, who hurries from one machine to the other, who avoids the crack in the platform. There is no more thought or feeling, or, at least, I'm not bothered by them any more: they have become objects of independent contemplation. In the end exertion itself ceases to exist: there is only a consciousness (or is it a memory?) of my exhaustion. I am aware of how great my tiredness is; I know that when I have finished this run I am going to feel exhaustion right in the marrow of my bones, and I know in advance that it will be hard for me to get the next batch going, and to drop back again into this same state. I am the rhythm of the machine, and this perhaps is why, of all else from the world outside work, it is sex – of the same inert, impersonal character – which finds a place in my consciousness. To make love without loving: the rhythm drives me on; I *know* what I feel and what I will feel, but I do not *feel* it.

When a thought materializes, against all odds, it cannot break lose. It is snapped up by the rhythm, and turns round, like a caged squirrel in a tread-mill. The most immediate, the latest, the most elementary rage or insult or aggravation is transformed into these pseudo-thoughts; feelings of happiness, never. They weave into the rhythm and, while the work is going relatively easily, they abate; when it becomes harder, they regain their strength, making me grit my teeth, as my muscles tighten. They throb like questions or exclamations which cannot be answered. Sometimes it is impossible to contain them from coming out in a loud shout. They streak out like a curse that only someone who always works close to you, or a friend, can understand. 'Why is it always *me* who gives way?', or 'If I hand in my notice, he'll screw up his eyes like in a horror film'. Obsessive thoughts burst out when stopped in their tracks by the completion of a piece; like savage music they accompany the movement which hurls the piece into the box. So long as there is another piece to start on, you cannot follow up these thoughts, and there is always another piece to start on.

When they introduced the two-machine system, the factory did not in the first place aim to double production. Before all else, they endeavoured to economize on wages. It isn't out of zeal that the rate-fixers mark on every possible job 'for two machines'. They know full well that a 'perfect' combination, which allows us to double production, is very rare. They count on the fact that we will not be able to carry out in parallel most of the work they have so marked. But that's in their interest too. Working on a typical, average combination, we produce little more than if we had worked straight through on one machine, but our wage doesn't reach what we would have earned on one machine alone.

Obviously, we have no standard for comparison, as the two-machine system has now become a self-evident part of our conditions of work. Everyone could make calculations on a scrap of paper, as I have done, or simply think about the disadvantages of working two machines, and then evaluate the difference in wages compared to a long-abandoned way of working. But he would only be wasting his time, because too many other factors come into play. The two-machine norm is also a norm; perhaps a piece-rate for one machine only exists so that, from time to time, they can overpay us?

The two-machine system can appear so commonplace that one's perception of what is 'paid' or 'unpaid' becomes relative. It's not only the two-machine system, but also wage-labour in general as well as piece-rates themselves, which are based upon the fact that the worker is prepared to maintain such relativity. In the final analysis, the intermingling of 'paid' and 'unpaid' work stems from the identity of piece-rates and forced labour. In our section, there's a worker who gets very obstinate from time to time. He is then quite capable of going as far as the works director to express his indignation about not being given a supplementary wage. 'I suppose they think I'm going to work for nothing!' He gets into one of these states so rarely that the foreman usually gives in. The same worker has toiled for years and years on two machines, for half pay, without a word of complaint.

We are like natives who, in the early days of colonialism, handed over everything, their treasures, their land, and themselves, for worthless trinkets and who became aware that they had been robbed only when they failed to get the usual junk in return.

We have no perception of this relationship, and yet we suffer from it. However well we are paid we still remain completely dissatisfied; the proof is that we are always ready to produce more for a little more pay, ready in fact to produce all that they tell us to. One might think that the two-machine system itself is so outrageous that it would shatter the illusion that we are really being paid, and with it the illusion of paid work in general. But the truth is that it enhances the power of the illusion. When it emerges that the two-machine system does not improve our pay in comparison with the old system, or with hourly wages, this does not appear to us as a brutal manifestation of the famous relations of production, we feel fucked: well and truly fucked.

[NOTE: I myself can only write about wage-labour, piece-rates, norms, supplementary wages, and the two-machine system as outrages. But, in putting the emphasis on their specific characteristics, I feel that I am guilty of maintaining the illusion that these are contingent forms which can be reformed. It seems to me that, right up to the blank page in front of me, money proves the omnipotence that it has already demonstrated in the factory. It not only has the capacity to guarantee or to threaten my existence, but also that of censuring my tongue. When I come to speak of it, I am incapable of finding words which would allow me to express anything which seems in any way adequate. Money exercises an absolute power over the terrain of objectivity: here, as in the factory, it has the power to exile into the realms of poems those who dream of abolishing it or—which comes to the same thing—to cut out their tongues. I was able to establish that my colleagues were capable of finding words for everything, except for one thing, which indisputably exists: this dream which expresses itself, in a stammering way, in those moments when all objectivity is lost.]

By the same token, unexpected windfalls have a completely disproportionate effect on us. For instance, sometimes newly designed pieces, marked for two machines by the office, are reallocated after a while 'for one machine', because in the meantime they have realized that no one could do them on two. The full pay which we get as a result seems like a present, since up until then we made this piece for half as much.

Examples of the opposite are more frequent, but with a little effort one learns not to take them too much to heart. Under the scheme of 'technical development' and 'maintenance of the norms' – two concepts which, together with 'organization of labour', were the catchwords for the introduction of the two-machine system – we sometimes receive a new locking device to take one of the few pieces 'for one machine' which still exist. With this new device you can handle more pieces than with the old one: it allows us to mill on automatic feed and means that we don't have to turn the table by hand. However, the time it takes to set everything up increases: there are more clamps on the apparatus, and you have to manipulate the bolts to get them in the best position. If we work solely on one machine, such a 'technological development' would not even be enough to diminish the piece-time. But since the piece is now marked for two machines, the time per piece is slashed in half. After the delivery of the new device, we get new money, marked 'T.g.r.: 2'.

Foremen hand out supplementary wages for work on one machine just as sparingly as they do for two. It doesn't bother them at all to concede openly that in *special* cases they pay for the other half of work we *always* do. Nonetheless, to get round it they resort to the strangest tricks of the trade.

One of the best, over which they took a lot of trouble, went as follows: At the beginning of my day's work, I receive a single large batch, marked 'for two machines', but not accompanied by another series. The foreman waits until I get started, in the hope that a supplementary wage is a certainty, then he has another batch sent over to me. He makes sure to keep himself well away from me. The dogged face of the labourer who brings it over shows that he is used to the machine-workers yelling at him 'Who told you to bring over this batch of shit?', although they know perfectly well who it was. No argument is possible: the supplement is off. On top of it all the second batch must remain untouched: if I interrupted the run which I've already begun in order to prepare the other machine, I would be even worse off.

The supplementary wage for 'one machine only' work must also be demanded, each and every time, although the foreman knows exactly what your situation is since he set it up in the first place. He pays great attention to the different kinds of combination he hands out when he divides up the work. If he doesn't like someone he arranges it so that he doesn't get work 'for one machine'.

They can't economize on the supplement for one-machine work – when they give it – since it isn't fixed according to their whims and fancies and can't be rounded off. It is exactly that necessary to raise half pay to full pay, less the few tenths of the multiplier. They don't even have to calculate it; they just look it up in a large register which tables the supplements in fillérs.

One could describe the supplement for 'one machine only' work as being incompatible with other sorts of supplementary wage. Quite simply, it is impossible to ask for two sorts of supplementary wages on the same day, however justified they may be. Even good old Gyuri shakes his head with dismay, and says, 'Aren't you claiming supplementary wages a little too often? We aren't a charity, you know.' Similarly, they won't tolerate our asking for supplementary wages too many days in a row. Supplementary wages are earned through fasting. The foreman urges abstinence and moderation on the insatiable supplement-earners.

The head foreman likes to play the guardian angel. 'By chance', he overhears an argument, listens to what both sides are saying, and then decides that, yes, this time a supplementary wage will be in order. 'But don't you make a habit of it, eh!' And one has to say thank you, just as you always have to thank them for everything, every payment, every signature. A 'thank-you' left unsaid, or a door slammed in an office, can cost you dearly.

The millers in the section aren't all equally good at looting on two machines. M and his shift-mate race through their runs with fury, shouting oath after oath. At every opportunity of supplementary wages, they come down heavily on the foreman; but, since their capacity is irreplaceable, most of the time – and sometimes day after day – they get their hands on 'good' work, batches that can be marked for one machine. That's the most the foreman can do for them, but, obviously, it doesn't satisfy their 'impossible' demands for supplementary wages.

My instructor, too, very often asks for supplementary wages. The inevitable refusals don't seem to affect his good humour, or to damage his sense of pride. He tries to get round the foreman with a lot of soft talk; but the foreman stays as hard as marble. When he does get a good batch he's as pleased as Punch and whistles hit tunes as he works. 'You've got no idea how much I'm going to loot out of this lot,' he shouts at me. But before long he's feeling the strain again.

His shift-mate is tiny. They had to fix a special platform for him. He's worked in a lot of factories, and isn't very fit physically. He can't really take working on two machines, and everyone expects him to leave soon. His work is a boon to the foreman, who doesn't care at all if the little man lowers the level of average output. He dumps on him all the left-overs, all of them two-machine pieces – 'the plague' as M calls them. He struggles on as best he can. He never dares to ask for a supplement, and probably wouldn't get one if he did: his batches are 'regular' work, marked for two machines – the fact that even a skilled miller like M could not possibly do these jobs on two machines is another story. Anyway, it's quite possible that he doesn't know that supplementary wages exist. He has never had any, so he may never have noticed that he works for half pay. The union never told him anything, and if we did, it was by chance.

From what I've seen, my shift-replacement puts up a grim and dogged fight against the system. On average, he makes around 1,900 forints, and he's pleased when he hits the 2,000 mark. There is nowhere else for him to go to.

He doesn't have any qualifications; until recently he worked on the land, and he's not young any more. 'Show me a place where there's less work,' he says to me. For many years he's been building his own house, the whole family work just for that. Two out of ten work for such a nest, which can take ten years or more. A couple will save for years until they have enough to start building and move in, and then more years to furnish and equip it. It's a never-ending business; by the time they think they have finished the place is already over-crowded. But at least they live under their own roof. These house-builders would gladly put up with a three-machine system, if that were physically possible. Who knows? Perhaps it is.

No one attaches special significance to the two-machine system, not even to the extent of checking their 'money' to see if it indicated whether the work series had to be done on two machines. The main reason is that not only the two-machine system, but also the nature of the work itself, seemed unchangeable. Anyone who kept reminding himself how much he was losing would find that he was hampering his work. M pointed out to me that the two-machine system isn't the only method they have of cheating us. 'Now take the turners. They are fully qualified workers; they only work on one machine; but they seldom earn more than we do. If they did, you can be sure that they'd find a way of fixing it – one machine and all – so that their pay soon fell back again. They've always got something up their sleeves. You can be sure of that.'

And so the workers don't think anything through. They put themselves in a position where they have to drag the maximum out of everything and loot on two machines. The turners looked on the miracles of M and his mates with the greatest deference, summed up in the expression, 'I could never do it.'

The turners are properly qualified workers, but that barely distinguishes them from the skilled millers. What we have in common is much more important: we are all piece-rate workers. That means the same thing for everyone. What's the use of having studied basic mathematics, followed by three years' training, if throughout the year you work to a norm on nothing but the same thirty or forty standard jobs. The peasant who comes into the factory from the land sooner or later picks up all the knowledge necessary for that.

Evidently, our common lot is not enough to turn into friendship even if we work at the same task. Should our section include fully qualified millers, they would certainly get – for identical work – a higher hourly rate than those who were just skilled workers. And if by chance this difference (which does not in fact exist) should escape our notice, the foremen would make it their business to remind us of it constantly, so that they could pay us less. There are several turners who are skilled but unqualified: they can do any job perfectly well, but they rarely get given 'good' work.

It was a turner who told me about the Holy Trinity of the piece-rate worker. We were well into overtime; in fact, it was our twelfth consecutive hour on the job, around one in the morning, when I broke a disc on the horizontal miller. I knew that the piece was pretty well finished; I knew that I had to stop the machine; but I acted too late. The blade drove into the tempered steel block. The steel let out a delicate but murderous vibration: I wrenched down the stop lever with a single pull, provoking a terrible noise. Jumping backward, I covered my eyes.

'That's enough for today. Tidy up, take a shower,' the turner who was working at the other end of the section shouted at me. Until then we had never exchanged a single word. The two other workers also doing overtime were already by my machine. The turner who had told me to go home asked for my number so that he could clock me out. He was an old man, slow-speaking, but still in good shape. Putting the broom into my hand, he said in a low voice, as if he was ashamed of being so solemn in front of the others, 'Those who will be piece-workers must understand that it takes three things: one must have knowledge, one must have will, and one must have endurance. That is the Holy Trinity.' Only then did the foreman emerge from his office.

THE management we know only from the factory journal, when photographs show them presiding over some solemn assembly or other, a top gathering of the Party or trade union. Their sphere of activity is hazy (the list of official positions is too long to grasp and changes very often; their announcements in the journal seem much of a muchness). The role of the managing director is the clearest of all: there's no one above him. But apart from him there are several other directors: we don't know exactly how many. Our factory is large; the journal often calls it 'one big family'; in such a big family, you're bound to have a lot of daddies.

The managing director's name is known by about half the workers; those of his helpers by only a handful. Very few know the names of the heads of departments and their assistants, just as the senior Party and trade-union functionaries are also little known – usually only by Party members. Not that the Party members have met them, but sometimes, during Party gatherings, they get hold of extra information, even if it's not very precise. It's thanks to them that we occasionally pick up something, other than what the foremen want us to know.

We see the senior executives in flesh and blood when they've got visitors – especially if they're foreigners. Then they all stroll through the huge hall of the factory. I wish that we could bring along students of drama to study the behaviour of those taking part in these rapid encounters. I would like them to see how *everyone* tries to appear *other* than he is. The most nervous workers suddenly begin to imitate the most poised characters, assiduous, detached and indifferent. The visitors put on masks of passionate interest and intense curiosity, restrained – alas – only by the brevity of their tour. As for the masters of the place, well, they exhibit a demiurgic pride in this animated, well-oiled spectacle.

Such observers would also have to note how hints of reality shoot through from behind the façades. Our work rhythm has relaxed. That comes from something more complex that the simple attempt to disguise passing curiosity behind half glances, carefully calculated movements, and the pretence of tidying up this and that. It's also the result of our confusion, itself provoked by contradictory feelings. We know that we are being shown to the visitors and, instantly, we see ourselves through their eyes. The insane rhythm of looting, celebrated up until the second of the visitor's arrival as the triumph of our own will, appears to us, suddenly, and with intolerable force, as the product of a zeal which is shameful, compelled, and circumscribed. Before we realize it we have already slowed down. We become, there and then, model workers with confident movements and calm demeanours, preoccupied with the work itself, without regard to the pay. The visitors also betray themselves, through unmistakable signs. Their flustered and distracted gaze as they go hither and thither, and the set smiles on their faces, witness their insoluble dilemma. They have not come to see round the factory on our account but only to convince themselves, as they round off their negotiations, that the factory exists, the machines are working, and that production is trouble-free. However, while they are actually in the workshop, they must show some interest in us. Their pained awareness of our presence elicits an exaggerated friendliness and benevolent curiosity, which does not extend to a single one of us individually.

When they have finished trekking around, the daily rhythm slowly starts to re-establish itself. As an epilogue to our previous confusion we exchange cynical comments which make fun of our visitors – their dress, their clumsiness and their embarrassment. But our laughter does not ring true.

We try to guess who was who. But they pass too quickly, and there are too many of them, even though we have been forewarned of their names and rank by the foreman, who rushes round beforehand; not in order to tell us who they are, but to get us to tidy things up a bit. He hustles the unskilled labourers, gets them to stop loading trolleys with new materials and to take up brooms instead. The narrow lanes between machines are cleared of pieces and, after that, the boxes are pushed out of the way. Finally, the head foreman makes a last quick check, an inspection of the course, and perhaps orders that a battered old hat be taken off the top of a milling machine, where to our amusement for the last three days it has danced on the spindle. The youngest unskilled labourers are packed off to some far corner, as far out of sight as possible: it is better that the visitors don't see them, even if the louts don't fool around.

When the visit is over, the foreman makes another round through the section: this time to accelerate the process of getting us back to our normal rhythm.

We have hardly any other contact with senior executives. Most of us arrive at the factory through a back entrance – the nearest to the tramway station – but those who go in through the main one can see them just before the afternoon shift. Usually they are getting ready to leave. Someone once saw a whole caravan of them. 'That was something. If only you had seen it. The whole gang came out, their cars lined up waiting for them, two Mercedes in front, and the Volgas behind. They slammed the doors one after the other, like a volley of machine-gun fire. The whole lot were rushing off somewhere.'

Once, at an *ad hoc* meeting, the foreman read out a personal appeal from the managing director, calling on us to make collective sacrifices. He, the foreman, interpreted this to mean that we would have to put in more overtime in order to get the profit-sharing bonus at the end of the year. But, at the end of that year, no such bonuses were distributed. The factory journal gave an astonishing explanation: 'In spite of production reaching the planned schedules, the money allocated for bonuses has already been spent in paying for overtime.'

If nobody had got dividends, then the workers would have done rather well: the loss of the few hundred forints which since the introduction of the economic reforms we'd got as our part of profit-sharing would be nothing in comparison with the loss that the workers' zeal for overtimewould have caused the bosses, above all the senior executives. But, as the annual profit-dividends for directors (10,000 forints for middle-rank executives, and hundreds of thousands for senior executives) have, over the past few years, been built into their monthly salaries, it is impossible to verify the rumours that this year as well, in one way and another, the bosses have done very well.

'Speaking for myself, I wouldn't mind a swop: they could have my little nothing, and I'd take theirs,' my neighbour said when he heard that there would be no profit-sharing at the end of the year.

The full-time union official who is responsible for the millers' section often takes part in production conferences: he was elected on the recommendation of the heads of the factory union by the section secretaries, but he wasn't one of them. He always intervenes, but what he says has only remote connections with reality; he returns time and time again to his pet themes. In particular, he loves repeating how several of the directors started out as workers.

In fact, the year before last there was still a grinder, since retired, who twenty-seven years ago worked with one of the bosses. When he started in the factory, the director-to-be was already there. Since then, a lot has happened: they went their separate ways. 'We often taunted the old chap, telling him to go and see his former colleague to chat him up and see if he couldn't fix up for him to become a deputy director. The old fellow himself always said, "A boss, what does it mean? In America, shoe-shine boys become millionaires. When he gets to be a millionaire – in dollars – then I'll go up and see him."' The worker who recalled all this concluded: 'In my opinion, the old fellow wasn't all there. I would have gone straight up and seen the bloke.'

THE rate-fixers I don't have much to do with. They have their place in the office building. None of the workers has ever set foot there. The rate-fixers appear in our section only when 'something is up'. This expression always reminds me of those characters who go out looking for a fight. Before swinging their punches, they provoke their would-be opponents by asking, 'What's up with you, then?'

The unexpected appearance of the rate-fixers is always a bad sign. It means that they are going to re-time a piece, or test some new machinery. Anyway, it always has something to do with our piece-rates, and they never go to the trouble of raising them.

They can also come on to the shop-floor when there's been a complaint. But none of these rare appearances has anything to do with what is called 'revision of the norms'. For that, there's no need for them to descend to the work-shop: it's enough for them every so often to lower the time per piece for most of our jobs, usually around once a year. It's easy work, clean, free of serious arguments, which does not demand that they have to breathe in the stifling stench of machine oil, or avoid showers of sparks and glowing swarf, or put up with the 'stupid' remarks and insults of the workers.

It isn't purely for reasons of comfort that they stay closeted in their office during a general revision of the norms. The argument which justifies these revisions is, in effect, that the average rate of production was too high; it has become evident that the norms are not tight enough. But they know very well that this thesis would be immediately demolished if they took stop-watch readings on piece after piece, down here on the shop-floor.

They always work under orders. At least, that is what they say to workers when they appear because 'something's up'. It's probably true concerning the revision of the norms, since the rate-fixers who come down to see us are young and recently qualified, and not the senior technicians who keep themselves out of the way. But re-timing a norm, and timing its rate for individual pieces, was a matter for their initiative. Their stop-watches tick away with real zeal: their promotion depends on it. Sharp eyes, firmness, an absolute insensitivity to evidence of the wounds they are inflicting on the enemy: those are the qualities rate-fixers need. 'Maintaining the norms' is a battle.

The workers on the machines seldom complain when the norm is impossible. Just so long as there remains a chance of looting, whether this means skirmishing with accidents or taking gambles on quality, they don't demand that the foreman should go and find a rate-fixer. Experience has taught them that a complaint in the case of one piece, which is crowned with subsequent success, is invariably followed by a reduction in the time allowed for others.

No one has ever divulged to the workers the principles governing the determination of the norms, but some have become clear to them through their own experience. Few workers consider the instant retaliation which follows a victorious complaint to be a matter of personal vengeance. They are well aware that the rate-fixers adjust the piece-rates by reference to an average – which explains why, when the correction of one norm is forced through, a deterioration in others follows automatically, even before the general revision of the norms. But the nature of this average is completely inscrutable. 'It's what they think is economic,' said my neighbour.

The rate-fixers lose no words over their principles. If you ask them for a stop-watch check on one of your pieces, they snarl at you, and reply curtly, 'You're very happy with the time on the other jobs, their times are good. You never make a fuss about them.'

Nevertheless, it does happen, very occasionally, that in spite of everything someone has a rate-fixer called in to check a particular job. He would not set out on this adventure, doomed to ultimate failure, unless he was given such a large number of the pieces concerned that the batch had too great an effect on his monthly pay. Such a prospect would be even more unbearable than the knowledge that what he was doing might mean, two months later, that he would have to accelerate the runs on other pieces even faster in order to make his living. Besides, it's quite possible that in the final reckoning the impersonal vengeance of the rate-fixers will not hurt him individually, or at least will not be directed at him alone, but will be spread out among all the machines doing the same type of work. A bitter consolation.

The first round is played out in the foreman's office. Several visits are needed before you eventually catch him when he is not on the telephone. Workers are not permitted to go straight to the rate-fixers.

At first, the foreman tries to discourage these requests, and sometimes he manages to do so; for example by promising to exchange the 'bad' batch for a 'good' series. The foreman doesn't like the rate-fixers' visits: they always lead to tension in the workshop; they disrupt the usual innocuous topics of conversation, and encourage even cautious workers to complain.

When the rate-fixer finally turns up, he shakes hands with the plaintiff, and the game begins in earnest – a battle conducted according to complex rules.

The worker who makes the rate-fixer come down earns little money. Even so, when he argues with the rate-fixers, the question of money doesn't come into it. The naked figures of the piece-time come to life, so that the warring parties seem to be motivated by a pure and disinterested love of truth; the whole discussion can pivot around tenths of a minute.

The rate-fixer's procedure is apparently correct: he doesn't just measure the time for a single piece, but lets ten, twenty or thirty go through and then takes the average. It's just that he stops his watch during every movement which he regards as superfluous, and sometimes he does so quite arbitrarily, should he feel that the work is going too slowly. He does not take account of time taken in preparation: studying the blueprint, choosing tools, setting the machine – not to mention all the moments inevitably lost during the unforeseeable hitches, inspection and conversation with the foreman.

Obviously the worker who made the complaint has some tricks of his own. The best is to *follow* the technical instructions, and make the machine run at the speed indicated. He also observes the safety regulations: he doesn't touch the table while the machine turns; he tightens all the bolts into their nuts; he sweeps up the swarf after each piece. But he doesn't take things too far: there's no question of him going to the foreman and asking for protective goggles. No one has seen even the smallest plexi-glass face-shield here; such a demand would sound like a declaration of intent – to sabotage.

You couldn't possibly say that he was working slowly (he would be too ashamed that the rate-fixer or the foreman at his side might upbraid him for that). On the other hand, he does not keep up that insane rhythm which alone permits him to earn his living. He works in the way that he would like to be able to work every day.

The rate-fixer is quite untouched by all this: he stops his watch mercilessly, when he sees fit. If the change-over of pieces seems a bit slow, he just ignores one in three. The time measured on the stop-watch is always less than the time taken as indicated by the factory clock. Even if he is convinced that the piece has been executed at the prescribed speed, the rate-fixer *knows* that the usual rhythm of work is always more rapid than that which he witnesses, and that's good enough for him.

'It's no good talking to them. They say to themselves "Now you're creeping forward like a sloth, but as soon as my back is turned, you'll be as quick as a weasel." And there's some truth in that. After all, they don't need to step out of their office, all they need to do is add up what I earn, they can't fail to notice that sometimes I produce in one hour what the norm stipulates should take two. Last month I had a whole week in which I clocked up, every day, at least 800 minutes of official piece-time. How can I look them straight in the eyes when I'm compelled to do these tricks to get money?' said one miller.

When a worker's complaint leads to a time-check on a given job, we usually find that a few days later a slight increase in the time prescribed for this piece is indicated on our pay slips. This isn't a matter of chance: those who make a complaint only do so if they are sure of their ground. They have carefully chosen the piece from the mass of jobs whose norms can never be realized. It isn't long before the benefits of this little victory vanish, but in defeating the rate-fixers they have discharged some of their rage.

The same thing happens in reverse – and more often – when the rate-fixers come down to the shop-floor uninvited, for example to try out some new clamping apparatus. Guided by the foreman, they pick out the most experienced worker from all those who have manufactured that piece before. They make him stop whatever he is doing, and the foreman promises him a supplementary wage for trying out the new apparatus. One could not say that this offer is especially well received. The new apparatus means that the piece-rate will drop, and the battle begins to keep the reduction as small as possible.

The rate-fixer doesn't even tell the worker who carries out the test what reduction he has in mind, for one thing because it is none of his business, for another because they modify the results in any way they like in the witches' cauldron of the rate-fixers' department. If they shared the final result of the test with the worker who made the piece, he could use it as a means of control over further pieces.

One day M's shift-mate was chosen to test a new machine. They told him that the piece-time was not going to be reduced. 'I should have known better what they were up to, but there was nothing in their faces to give them away. In two days new "money" came out. The piece had been reallocated "for two machines". I was so beside myself that old Gyuri wanted to send me home, I'd been taken in completely.'

He was quite right: he should have known what they were about, because the rate-fixers do not reckon that the division of both pay and piece-time by half represents a reduction. Which means they can say, pointing to the other machine, 'You can work on the second one as well, while this job is going through.'

If they were interested, they could easily satisfy themselves that the two-machine system rarely allows for a perfect combination. And even when that does happen it doesn't affect the fact that we do double work for the same pay. But the whole thing is a mockery when they come down and time on one machine a norm that will in fact have to be met while working on two.

In the official jargon of the time-keeper's office, the word *norm* never appears. They talk about 'technology', 'production technology', and the like. This makes their work appear to be a technical business, indispensable to production. Effectively, they are the ones who break down into thousands of isolated movements all the tasks carried out in this enormous factory. For them to believe in their mission it must be cracked up to be the best, the most rational process of determining production. In fact, they're there to work out the method which will yield the biggest profit. The technical solution which they select is subordinated to a single goal: that all the workers, on each and every one of the machines, should furnish the maximum output in exchange for the minimum possible pay. In the final analysis, their function is to find that technology which will permit the maintenance of our wages – and of wages in general – at a level which has been predetermined. When they break down the processes of manufacturing a product into movements and operations, they're not only trying to make maximum use of the machines, and maximum economies with the materials – but also the cheapest and most effective utilization of the workers. Our wages must follow on our slightest movements, and our thinking be bound to the wages we receive. Our thoughts are, in a certain sense, programmed to oscillate incessantly between momentary satisfaction and the necessity of starting all over again the following day: they are always directed towards production. The technology is planned in such a way that it turns us – we who put it to work – into its slaves and enemies.

The technology of the norms is a miraculous technology.

From the labour of those who know only fragments, it welds a totality; and it realizes a finished product from the labour of men who do not know the purpose, either of the product, or of their own labour, and whose aim is to maintain their existence. In ever-increasing quantity technology creates quality from the work of men for whom quality is an enemy, and quantity a torment; it becomes acceptable to men who can know no more about it than that it allows them to produce the cost of perpetuating themselves.

He who sells his time, his strength, his abilities for wages, whether bit by bit for piece-rates or in a more transparent, total form, knows that he does not work for himself. He knows that he has sold everything, including his right to determine how much he will produce. The norm is nothing other than the quintessence of those connections between men that the social scientists call the relations of production in wage labour. Under favourable circumstances the wage can be adequate, even generous: the norm, never. The norm is the thinly veiled constraint within the apparently voluntary framework of wage labour. Incessantly it reminds those who dream of a fair wage of the true nature of wage labour, so that as a result of the constant threat to our conditions of life, we 'freely' pave the way to ever-growing output. The norm is a shameless admission of cynicism: whose creators have no interest in production as the fruit of the living will of workers.

In a book which came out in 1960 it is stated that the workers have always used moments of political tension or confusion to force down the norm – for example in 1953 or 1956. On the other hand, the first step towards political stabilization has always been the re-establishment and enforcement of the norm (András Hegedüs,* *The wage system in our industry*, p. 94). Anyone who works in a factory knows, without need of statistics, that for those who work to norms, complex arguments about whether or not they own the means of production are nothing but empty talk. Such

*Hegedüs was briefly prime minister before 1956 and subsequently became a sociologist. He was expelled from the Communist Party in 1973.

arguments merely allow them to feed on their typical, bitter, self-destructive ridicule.

The system of norms is far more effective at shackling the imagination than at stimulating production: the most daring dream of piece-rate workers is to achieve a fair and sufficient hourly wage: in other words, to be delivered from the norm. If a utopia of productive relations where they could determine their goals together threatens to break to the surface, they immediately force it back.

'When I retire, then perhaps I'll have the time to speculate about such nonsense. You and I will never have the power to say how much we should work. There'll always be someone who gives the orders. That's how it always has been, and that's how it always will be,' M was curtly told by his shift-mate. The vague thought which had made him flare up was contained within one of the most frequent of all complaints. M had said that the rate-fixers didn't really understand their jobs; they knew nothing about the true capacities of the machines or the tricks of the trade. He had simply stated that 'production would get along much better if we had a say in fixing the norms'. He added, 'Those characters spend all their time dreaming about how much they can lop off our piece-times. The devil help them, they can shit around on their own.' That was all it took to enrage his shift-mate.

Each new increase in output extracted by the norms excites pain and anger in us. But does the norm really get the most out of us?

The rate-fixers like to see themselves in the role of technicians who, with exact 'scientific' methods, follow the level of technological development and set out the possible ways of increasing production. In fact, they are groping around in the dark, they raise the norms at random, and modify them if they don't work out. As for quality, they must call in others to enforce it – the inspectors, in fact, who have no other function.

They don't even need to admit what everyone knows, namely that they can't count on any information coming from us, who actually operate the machines. On the contrary, the whole of their 'science' is aimed at overcoming our instinctive, unremitting sabotage. Perhaps, in some places, this enemy science really does have the means of escaping sabotage, and reckoning what we are capable of, here and now, as wage workers, implementing an alien will. But it has no idea of what we would or could do in its place, on our own account. Our sabotage is nothing other than a refusal to give away our knowledge and experience: the form which it takes is to falsify them. But can one still talk of being scientific when the workers see science as their enemy? We haven't the slightest interest in the possibilities of rationalization, and if we ever became aware of them, and put them to use, we conceal the fact. We reduce the effectiveness of new technology as much as we can, and we sabotage its further development.

My workmates don't think much of measures taken to alleviate work, because they're always accompanied by an increase in production, or at least a reduction in pay. The technology of norms has absolutely no place for methods which lessen the compulsion to produce without also cutting back wages. If they could invent a new machine that was less demanding, the worker would have to service three at the same time; when an apparatus is introduced which requires only half an hour's work, someone will have to do this half-hour as part of what he's doing already. The eight hours must be worked without rest or respite. The first goal of a technical science under the control of workers would be an increase in production that reduced the amount of work necessary to bring it about. Of course, that would be possible only if what happens to profits also came under their control.

This whole science of norms comes down to this: that production extracted under the yoke of wages is transformed – through exact methods – into a new wage-rate, and the results of this technical science, which has been financed by the workers' labour, are forced upon those who, without it, would be the best friends of science.

It is hard to suppress the thought that the relationship between us and our bosses, culminating in the norm, is not an inducement, but on the contrary, the biggest possible obstacle to the development of human, useful, production. The greatest miracle which the norm effects is that it manages to increase production at the same time as it strips it of meaning and of its principal driving force: the identification of the worker with the goals of his own production.

General revision of the norms bursts the ulcer of the norms and the whole system of factory production. The entire factory is raked over, not a moment's sleep is lost over the harm done to wages – and workers – as the new order is applied, not by a simple reduction but through a general tightening of norms. The only possible means of defence is to hand in your cards. Those who feel that with the new norms they won't manage to maintain their former pay, even if they intensify their work, give in their notice, as do those who can no longer physically withstand the new rhythm of work. And so, to avoid waves of quitting which inevitably follow, they rarely proceed with an all-in revision of norms; they much prefer to implement progressive tightening, section by section, task by task. According to the oldest and most experienced workers, they try to co-ordinate general adjustments with the other factories, to throw a chain of synchronized revisions around those tempted to flee. Such collaboration is rendered possible by the fact that the setback or crisis which provokes a general revision of the norms usually affects more than one factory at a time.

But the last full-scale revision in our factory came at a moment when they could not have taken account of the situation in other factories. That year the newspapers proudly proclaimed that the increase in total national production was solely due to mounting productivity (which means that the same number of workers produced more. Did their wages rise in proportion?). Our factory, however, was not struggling for an increase in profits, but for profits as such, for sheer survival. The gravity of the situation required severe remedies.

Two or three years ago, in our factory as in many others, they decided to give us every other Saturday off, which meant that our working time was reduced by four hours a week. Our pay was not supposed to change. That proved no problem, of course, for monthly salaries, nor for hourly wage rates, to which they just added the rate for four extra hours a week; but for piece-rate workers, it called for something more complicated. They had calculated that the reduction in working time reduced the earnings of piece-rate workers by an average of 9·1 per cent. The wages department therefore added a sum corresponding to 9·1 per cent to the workers' pay.

For three years there was no problem about this; everyone was happy with it. Until, that is, they used the occasion of the fresh revision of the norms to announce that 'this deplorable state of affairs will finally cease'. Piece-rates would be changed: every *piece-time* would go up by 9·1 per cent and the compensation for free Saturdays would be done away with.

The workers sensed that they were being cheated, and reacted with unexpected violence. Our passionate discussions led M and some others to make an intervention at the production meeting, in the requisite form, that is, through a *question*. They said that the staff in the wages department should not risk straining their wrists by giving an extra crank to their adding machines. If they really had to solve the thing this way they didn't have to raise the piece-rate by raising the time-rate, it would be simpler to raise the basic rates of pay. Couldn't they do that equally well because the increase was a formal matter? 'How can they raise the time per piece on paper when the rate-fixer has already determined it with his stop-watch?' M asked, to murmurs of approval. The workers suddenly had good reason to defend the times per piece which, until then, they had always regarded – rightly – as a farce.

At the end of production conferences, those who ask questions have the right to respond. The head foreman had said that he could not really understand what the 'questions' were, since, in fact, nothing was going to change: the 9·1 per cent hitherto added on every month would now be integrated into every batch of pieces. He didn't waste a word in defence of the method by which piece-times are fixed, which had been unmasked yet again. His reply was met with silence: any further objection would have been out of place. The necessary information had been put to the meeting: 'The workers were informed in detail, and have been consulted in the preparation of decisions.' At least, that's what the factory journal said after the production conferences in all the sections were over.

The reason why M and his colleagues had protested is that they saw in advance what the practical effects of this 'solution' would be. The only way to tighten the norm is to reduce the piece-time, which automatically produces a reduction in the pay per piece. M and the others feared that the apparent increase in the piece-time would only lead to its subsequent cutback and therefore also in the norm; a straightforward increase in piece-rates would make this much more difficult.

Then came the big fiddle. Our new money appeared. Sensational: nothing, or almost nothing, had changed. In certain cases the time per piece had been brought down a little, in others it had been put up a bit.

What had happened? Quite simply, they had introduced *at the same time* the (formal) increase in piece-times of 9·1 per cent corresponding to the free Saturday, and a (real) revision of the time-norms of, on average, 10 per cent. The end result of the operation was to rob the piece-rate workers of theirl pay for their Saturday off.

Most of them had long since robbed themselves of this free day: they worked overtime. By working on both free Saturdays, they could do a total of sixteen hours overtime. That would have brought them additional income, but under the new system it was just enough to get them back to what they'd been earning before. 'Overtime is purely voluntary,' announces the foreman, when he walks round at the beginning of the month with his note-book to take the names of those who commit themselves to so many hours.

In the workshop there are cautious, serious and discreet discussions about whether it would be worth leaving, and the chances of finding jobs in other, 'better' places. The caution is well founded. Recently, the chief sent for two turners and they came out of his office with red faces. No one asked them then and there what it was all about. Later they replied to our questions laconically, shrugging their shoulders. 'He said that he did not tolerate propaganda and that we were only here to produce, as if we didn't know it.'

In spite of everything, the first notices to quit began to come in. The factory journal set about publishing articles on loyalty to the factory, cartoons about 'migrating birds' and photos of the model workers, weighed down with their medals. And for good measure, stressed the recent Budapest decree warning that workers can be subject to forced labour if they wish to leave their jobs after working in one place for less than a year.

'HOMERS? Is there any chance of homers?' is often asked by those thinking of leaving, when they're tipped off about another place. Many factors must be taken into account when you want to change your job. Although for most workers homers are not vital, they'll make them if they have the chance, and they'll try to create the opportunity if it doesn't exist already. Some will pay a high price to obtain a position which allows them to make homers.

The satirical journals portray workers who make homers as thieves. Similarly, the factory bosses 'fight' against homers. Warnings and sanctions rain down on the heads of those who misappropriate materials, use machines for their own purposes, or tap the factory's supply of electricity. If the factory guard finds a homer in our pockets or on our bodies, he has caught a thief.

But even if the satirical journals don't realize it, both workers and bosses know very well this is just words. The real damage to the factory is the time lost in making an object – time which cannot be utilized by the factory. 'If "The Accordionist" knows you're doing homers, he'll send a labourer to fetch some glue and he'll stick you to your machines for the rest of the day,' said my neighbour, joking with someone who was borrowing a tool from him to make a homer.

The secret of this passion for homers is not a simple one. It can't be reduced to the minimal value of the knick-knacks which the workers actually make and, especially on piece-rates, how long they take bears no relation to the value of the time lost.

Workers on hourly wages turn to homers when they have given to the factory what the factory has demanded, or when they have a free moment. If hourly workers make homers they don't risk anything – except being found out. Not only will they then be punished, the discovery will also offer an excellent opportunity to demand increased production from them.

Workers on conveyor belts, or on fully automatic machines, completely delivered from the pressures of time, are only likely to make homers in their dreams. Technological development has given these workers a moral superiority, which at least forces the satirists to look for a new theme in their attacks.

But the piece-rate worker manages his time himself, and each minute that passes without an increase in the number of pieces represents a loss for him. With the constant pressure of piece-rates, the factory does all it can to preach the morality of labour. According to the rate-fixers' estimates, the piece-rate workers should themselves renounce their passion for theft. In fact, management has to admit that nothing – neither prohibitions, nor punishments, nor public humiliation by the security guards – will persuade them to give it up.

Perhaps it is more than an empty play on words to say that we loot in order to have time to steal.

Making homers is a real addiction; those who go in for it know that they do themselves more harm than good. The bosses and the rate-fixers view the persistent refusal of piece-rate workers to give up this habit in terms of the basest instincts. 'How does a person like that bring up his children? We gave him sound advice and even delivered a sharp rap across his knuckles, but nothing will stop him from pilfering,' the foreman grumbles, talking about a homer addict. Yet the passion for looting does not upset the bosses. Not because they compel us to do it, but because looting doesn't cost anything except the strength, nerves, well-being, thoughts and life of the worker – even when he thinks that he is stealing something from the factory.

Why, then, are piece-rate workers so fond of making homers? The usefulness of homers cannot be the real motive, because the worker's life is so dependent on the workshop, the machine, his materials, and his eight-hour shifts that there is no chance whatever of his making anything which he really needs. It would be a dubious triumph for 'do-it-yourself' – given the gigantic level of infringe-ments that would be involved – if the conditions of work were such that they permitted workers to make everything they needed for setting up house in the form of homers. Then, certainly, homers would be worthwhile, since every worker could do repairs, and make small gadgets cheaply and with little effort.

Some of my colleagues still harbour a nostalgia for the days of the domestic artisan, but they rarely talk about their feelings, except when they are embarrassed or are making an excuse if someone catches them out. 'Peasants, too, give what they produce to the State, but they don't buy their vegetables in a market. Here, there are all the tools you could want, and stacks of discarded materials – but if I want to repair my tap, I'm supposed to call the plumber.' This sort of talk is really a rationalization; it doesn't bear much relation to the real motives for making a homer.

Perhaps the mechanics and fitters, who are paid by the hour, really do have the means – thanks to homers – to set up their families, since they have at their fingertips, in the workshop, all the tools and machines necessary for house-hold repairs large and small. But I am chained to my machine even if, at the most once a week, I find after an interminable number of runs that I have won a little time for myself. It is impossible for the piece-rate worker to flit across the workshop like a butterfly and to fiddle around with other machines. The foreman would see him at once, and fix him up with more work. Besides, the others are also riveted to their machines, and finally, our machines are too specialized, too large, too powerful and too complicated: they themselves dictate what we can make with them.

And so homers in fact are seldom useful things. Bizarrely enough, when they are, it is generally not for some outside use, but for something needed within the factory. In theory, there are special workers to manufacture the base plates and braces for mounting pieces, but in fact we must make them ourselves. It is an unwritten rule that when feasible we make everything our jobs require with our own machines. Such operations have real utility but are also infuriating. They are hardly paid but they make it possible to get through faster, or even complete a job.

Even around such necessary preparatory work, the mysterious aura of homers begins to appear, to the extent that everyone calls these pieces 'homers' even though in fact they entitle us to a supplementary payment. No one would think of telling his neighbour how he'd run through a series, and no one would be interested if he did. But everyone can talk with gusto about these preparatory 'homers', and find an interested audience. Without doubt, the reason is that we plan this work ourselves, and can complete it as we think best.

Our machines rarely give an opportunity for other useful kinds of homers. But that doesn't do away with homers, it only changes them. For piece-workers, homers are ends in themselves, like all true passions. Here the passion is for nothing other than work, work as an end in itself. The diverse forms of homer have only one thing in common: they have to be of a size that can be surreptitiously smuggled out of the factory. Some have not kept to this rule; and finished objects lie gathering dust in their locker, or their tool boxes, or besides their machines, until the worker changes his factory, when they try to get them out, or, if this is hopeless, give them away.

For us, the potential of milling machines, lathes and borers stimulates and at the same time limits our imagination. The raw material is chiefly metal. The objects that can be made are key-holders, bases for flower-pots, ashtrays, pencil boxes, rulers and set squares, little boxes to bring salt to the factory for the morning break, bath mats (made out of rolls of white polystyrene), counters in stainless steel to teach children simple arithmetic (a marvellous present), pendants made from broken milling teeth, wheels for roulette-type games, dice, magnetized soap-holders, television aerials (assembled at home), locks and bolts, coat-holders for the changing-room cupboard, knives, daggers, knuckle-dusters, and so on.

In place of the order, 'You make that', comes a question, 'What can I make?' But if this work is an end in itself, it is not thereby without a purpose. It is the antithesis of our meaningless 'real' work: the possibilities are limited, but the worker who makes a homer uses his head and keeps his eyes open. He scans the raw materials around him, weighs up the unexploited capacities of his machines and the other auxiliary machines, like the small disc-cutter in the corner of the section, or the grinding-machine, as he examines the hand tools at his disposal. Then he decides. He decides on what he will accomplish and works to realize that chosen object and not for some other purpose. If he uses the product itself, then before all else he will relish the pleasure of having accomplished it, and of knowing when, how, and with what he made it, and that he had originated its existence.

This humble little homer, made secretly and only through great sacrifices, with no ulterior motive, is the only form possible of free and creative work – it is both the germ and the model: this is the secret of the passion.

The tiny gaps which the factory allows us become natural islands where, like free men, we can mine hidden riches, gather fruits, and pick up treasures at our feet. We transform what we find with a disinterested pleasure free from the compulsion to make a living. It brings us an intense joy, enough to let us forget the constant race: the joy of autonomous, uncontrolled activity, the joy of labour without rate-fixers, inspectors, and foremen.

A complex organization compels me to maintain a minimum level of quality in my daily work. In making homers, quality, which itself arises as I have envisaged it, is the aim itself, the profit, and the pleasure. It is so natural that the question is no longer 'What are you making?' but 'How are you making it?'

The joy of this unity between conception and execution stands in extreme contrast to our daily work. 'Where is the blueprint?' an inspector asked as usual when he came over to make a check. M loves to repeat the brazen response (fortunately it did not get him into trouble) which aimed to rub in that for once he and the inspector had nothing to say to each other: 'It is here, in my head.' The inspector had to puzzle over this for a while before it clicked. M was making a homer. In outward appearance, nothing had changed. The same movements, which otherwise served only to increase production for the factory, were transformed by what he was doing into an activity of an entirely different kind.

By making homers we win back power over the machine and our freedom from the machine; skill is subordinated to a sense of beauty. However insignificant the object, its form of creation is artistic. This is all the more so because (mainly to avoid the reproach of theft) homers are rarely made with expensive, showy or semi-finished materials. They are created out of junk, from useless scraps of iron, from left-overs, and this ensures that their beauty comes first and foremost from the labour itself.

Many do not care if their noble end-product clearly reveals its humble origins; but others hold fervently to the need for a perfect finish. Were it not that homers have to be made in a few snatched minutes, and that often we can't get back to them from one week to the next, if making homers were not such a fleeting activity, then one could almost claim that there were two schools: the first 'functionalist', the second 'secessionist'.* There are also passing fashions in homers. And just as homers are a model of non-existent joys, so they are the model for all protest movements.

Making homers is the only work in the factory which stands apart from our incessant competition between each other. In fact it demands cooperation, voluntary cooperation – not just to smuggle them out but also to create them. Sometimes my neighbour asks me to do the necessary milling for his homer, and in return has made a support for me on his lathe. On these occasions we wait patiently until the other 'has the time'. Among piece-rate workers altruism is rare. Even in making homers, aid without a return is inconceivable. But it is not a matter of like for like: no one calculates how much his help is worth, or the time spent on it. *Sometimes* one can even come across selflessness

*An Austro-Hungarian movement of the beginning of this century, which celebrated excessive decoration.

without any expectations of recompense – which could never happen in 'real' work. Most friendships begin with the making of a joint homer.

The joys of 'the different' are obviously marred by the knowledge that they are only the joys of an oasis in a desert of piece-rates. Slowly, the factory returns to itself, the computer dries out the oasis, the pressures of production wax unchanged. Despite this, everyone is cheerful during these few precious minutes. This is manifestly obvious to all but the bosses – who don't need to worry about the constant bad temper of piece-rate workers except in so far as it relates to production; and who don't display the least understanding of this loophole to happiness, not even as a matter of tactics. A foreman's anger is a sure indication of the happiness which the worker sows with a homer.

I am convinced that homers carry a message. 'Artisanal tinkering, survivals from a dying industry: if homers are a negation, then they are only a nostalgia for the past.' This might be said if you didn't grasp the importance of homers for workers on piece-rates. In fact, they don't know the old handicrafts any more and they detest the private customers for whom many often do black labour after factory hours.

Workers would gladly renounce the artisan character of homers but they have no other way to assert themselves over *mechanized* labour. Similarly, they would gladly produce things which made sense, but the production of senseless homers is their only chance to free themselves, for a few minutes, from the 'good sense' of the factory. They would gladly manufacture, often collectively, things which were useful for the community; but they can only make what they want to make on their own, or at most with a few others.

So these two steps towards the senseless – producing *useless* things and *renouncing payment* – in fact turn out to be two steps in the direction of freedom, even though they are swiftly blocked by the wall of wage labour. In fact, homers are a vain attempt to defect from the cosmos of piece-ratios.

Suppose the whole of our work could be governed by the pleasures of homers, then it would follow that in every homer is the kernel of a completely different sense: that of work carried out for pleasure. The industrial psychologist, a petty juggler of the science of 'human relations', the expert in managerial methods, the social technician, and all the growing number of specialists who are replacing functionaries once breathless with the heroism of labour cannot comprehend the hopelessness of their task if they are unable to understand the pleasures of homers. Their task is to dry out the oases while filling the desert with mirages. Were it not that these experts in production are also dispensers of our livelihood, in command of discipline and achievement, we would enter the age of the Great Homer. This alienated sense, imposed from outside by wages (and its denial, the consolations of forbidden irrationality), would be replaced by the ecstasy of true needs. Precisely what is senseless about homers from the point of view of the factory announces the tranquil insistent affirmative of work motivated by a single incentive, stronger than all others: the conviction that our labour, our life, and our consciousness can be governed by our own goals. The Great Homer would be realized through machines, but our experts would subordinate them to two requirements, that with them we make things of real utility, and that we are independent of the machines themselves. This would mean the withering of production controls. We would only produce what united homer-workers needed and what allowed us to remain workers united in the manufacture of homers. And we would produce a thousand times more efficiently than today.

To take the whole world into account, to combine our strength, to replace rivalry with cooperation, to make what we want, to plan and execute the plans together, to originate what in itself would be our enjoyment simply because it existed; to be freed from the duress of production and its inspectors – all these are announced by the message of the homer, of the few minutes which resurrect our energy and capacities. The Great Homer would not carry the risk of our frittering away strength senselessly; on the contrary it would be the only way to discover what is even precluded by the homer of wage-earners: the real utility of our exertions. If we could direct our lives towards the Great Homer, we would gladly take on a few hours of mechanized labour a day, so long as it was needed. Otherwise, if everything remains as it does today, we face a terrible destiny: that of never knowing what we have lost.

Connoisseurs of folklore may look on homers as a native, decorative art. As yet, they aren't able to see further than that. But they will, and the day will come when homers are no longer forbidden but are commercialized and administered. People who work on automatic machines will be able to buy homers in the shops after seeing them in magazines, or on television. Then, no one will suspect that homers were originally more than a 'do-it-yourself' hobby, of a kind, or a mere pastime; that they once shone through factory controls, the necessity of making a living, and the pressures of wages, as a surrogate for something which by then perhaps will be even more impossible to name than it is today.

THE factory extends around me like a back-drop. I seldom perceive it as a whole, and I can hardly fit together the few details which I know. Where am I? Who am I? Is it really possible to get men in their right minds to accept this kind of life: to get them to come through a huge door, to cross these enormous workshops, to stand between neighbouring positions, to run through prescribed work, to bargain over the price of sweat, to collect a wage fixed by others, to go home and then return the next day to exactly the same situation? Is it really possible to make them believe – here, at home, everywhere – the assertions in the subtitles of this alien film, that everyone must accept what is beyond the comprehension of their senses, that we must live like this?

The same things are always painted on the back-drop, which is sometimes shifted around, but never enough to let me see the whole stage, or those who are running the show. Everyone has his own bit of scenery on which he chooses to see different things; every day he plays the same part over and over again with the same few actors. I have always wanted to stroll through the factory without any apparent purpose, to get to know others and to find out what they do. It would be good to follow a few of my pieces right through, to where they are fitted finally, and even further to the point at which they are used, and also along the journey they took to reach me in the first place. That wouldn't change much, but at least it would allow me to check a few of the things they throw in our faces as irrefutable arguments when we are given orders. If we could all do this, they couldn't shut us up so often with: 'That's the way it is; there's no alternative.'

But even this is just a dream, because here I am, stuck in front of my machine, bound hand and foot by piece-rates. Workers on the conveyor belt and those who run the automatic machines are tied by the machines themselves, the rest by discipline.

Should I arrive before my shift, the security guard would stop me, telephone my foreman, and I would only be allowed to cross the threshold of the factory with his permission. Similarly I come under suspicion if I leave late. There are two legitimate reasons for leaving late: 'voluntary work', that is political duties, and overtime. In both cases you must have a sanction signed by the foreman which you give to the security guard as you leave.

The very idea that the foreman would give me permission to wander about the factory without a definite reason and without supervision is ridiculous. Perhaps I could lie and say that I had something to do in one of the offices? But there is a foreman in every section, and each would stop me and ask what I was up to.

In fact, I don't even know my own section properly. Once or twice a day I trudge through it, carrying a heavy, oily milling head on my shoulder, which I change in a little store at the end because its teeth are broken, burned out, or worn away. But even if I wanted to, I couldn't look around: the heavy burden keeps my head rigid; if I turn it, I hurt my shoulder. Anyway I'm not anxious to look around; I have to change tools in 'my own time'. So I stare at my feet on the oily concrete. I can only reflect upon the foreman's pride, which he goes on about like a schoolmaster at every opportunity. Yes, it is justified: our labourers paint the borders between the rows of machines a lot better than they do in other sections. Twice a week, the sinister cortege puts in an appearance; two men carry the long marker, a third, the youngest, brings up the rear with a bucket full of lime. 'The artists are coming!' Sooner or later the head foreman appears as well to cast his protective shadow over this apparently senseless work, and the remarks cease. At the next production meeting the head foreman will not fail to emphasize, yet again, the deep significance of this drawing of the frontiers: 'an initiative', as he calls it, which makes an exemplary impression upon visitors 'from higher levels', and 'that benefits all of us'.

What I mainly know of our hall, and even of my own section, is a network or atmosphere – like the impression of an incomplete mosaic of moods and experiences. Each piece of this mosaic is a world in itself, where men pass half their lives, and from which, in turn, my machines are only a fleeting impression.

The section offices are in a wooden hut with large windows looking out across the shop floor. There, each worker has a pigeon-hole where we keep all our monthly pay-slips. I always have a quick look at my personal number: 101 091. The secretaries are curt and unsmiling with me, bantering with the foremen, and long-winded and obsequious with the head foreman. In one corner of the office is a large bottle of mineral water, crowned with an upside-down mug. They put it there for the summer, and change it when it is empty. That takes quite a while because the water is warm and flat. Those who work at the other end of the section don't come and get drinks here. 'By the time I get back to my machine, I feel thirsty again,' they say.

The walls of the office are covered with certificates. On top of the filing cabinets, embalmed in dusty cellophane, there are little flags, awarded as prizes. A portrait of Lenin hangs in the foreman's office, along with a photograph of the factory without a person in it, and some charcoal drawings. The first time I went into his office this little notice was already stuck on the door: 'For the expansion of trade union democracy with the election of management' – what could that possibly mean? They must have stuck it up there for some election or other and then forgotten all about it.

The foreman's changing-room is like a large cupboard. They put their work overalls on over their normal underwear. They've got a cracked washbasin between piles of old papers. The inspectors change with us, but they would gladly exchange the pleasure of our real showers for that meagre trickle of water. It's a question of prestige.

There is a worn, rickety table from which we can take pieces of classroom chalk without having to account for them. We don't need them much for our work – it is easier to judge the cutting depth if you pencil the mark against a white background – but we use them a lot more for throwing around. It's a diversion not confined to youngsters. A flick costs no time and the amusement of hitting your selected target can be shared with those you've alerted to your friendly assault. No one can get angry about it, and retaliation is expected once the culprit has been discovered. We've hardly any other need for pieces of chalk. Some use them to write up slogans in support of their favourite football teams, or the results of important matches, on the safety guards which protect us from flying swarf. In the filthy toilets –, those with strong legs crouch over them rather than sit down – the self-censorship slackens off. There's an ambiguous proclamation on the grey walls, 'Today 150 per cent!' Most graffiti leave it at the innuendo. Here, as well, are the odes to sexual misery which pass down from generation to generation.

The checking-in clock and the racks of time-cards are attached to the dirty walls by the entrance. Everyone knows to the second how this clock ticks. If I turn up at the factory gate at six o'clock, I am already late, since the check-point is the section itself and anyway the clock is a minute fast – something which certainly gives me back a minute at the end of the day, but that isn't the same. If you arrive late, you are fined, and your fines are docked from your pay at the end of the month. But this seldom occurs because the setters are so reluctant to help that we usually turn up 15–20 minutes ahead of time. 'The Accordionist' is always punctual and starts his round before the clock turns six; those who arrive late have to track him down to get work.

Up above, along the three sections of the huge hall, there are crane bridges – one large and two small – and in each section three mobile cranes as well. We operate the small cranes ourselves with a cable governor, although this is officially forbidden. Who can afford to wait around for the operators? Those who work in the centre section are forced to wait, because they can't climb into the crane's nest themselves. Fortunately for them, the operators really like this work; it must be amusing to find oneself up there, going backwards and forwards. Sometimes it's hard to persuade them to come down again. When they pass overhead, the cranes cast their shadows across us, the concrete floor and the machines tremble.

The final inspection point is separated off by an iron grill. Its enormous measuring table is wonderfully smooth, like a frozen lake of steel. Whenever I pass it I always give it a caress.

The service sections are against the walls. The tool shop with its opaque window. At the start of work, there's always a queue of people there, impatiently waiting for blueprints, micrometers, matrices, and slide-gauges. To guarantee the return of this material, we leave our factory-card on deposit: it has to be presented the next day at the factory entrance.

The darkly lit equipment store is the place of past and future milling apparatus. The older appliances bear traces of minor modifications, and forbidden 'inventions' made without the knowledge or permission of the rate-fixers. How these speeded up the runs was known only by the inventor, his shift-mate, and maybe a few friends. These marks are a clue to the foremen and the rate-fixers that technology can develop in other ways than through them and for their requirements. Just as with the joy of homers, the initiative does not last long: when they discover one of these secret inventions, which is probably mounted and detached daily, they cut the time per piece haphazardly. They know that officially investigating the times would be futile.

The tool store is on the opposite side, hewn out of the thick wall like a priest-hole. It is run by a young woman, nervous and suspicious. When she opens her window, the draught almost howls it's so great. Everyone can see how she suffers, but I'm afraid my shift-mate wasn't joking when he said, 'Too bad, it'll make her hurry when she hands out the tools.'

The grinding shop shelters the professional secrets of the turners. Each of them has his own little gimmick for sharpening his blades; every minute which the cutting edge can sustain counts. The grinding stones turn for a long time after their motors have stopped; dirty cooling water slops around in tin containers. A solitary pair of protective goggles, the glass broken, dangles from a plastic strap. On the walls, two posters repeat that the wearing of protective goggles is compulsory.

High up, above the cranes, are leaning accordion-windows, the symbol of all factories. (Why are these roofs the symbol, and not the stop-watch of the rate-fixers?) In summer the sun's rays pierce the dusty air, and from underneath all one can see are the clouds of rust which glisten in the vibrations of the overheated atmosphere.

The mercury vapour lamps are turned off in the morning, and not turned on until the afternoon. Everyone knows where the switch is, but it is the foreman's sovereign right to decide if it is dark enough to turn them on again. Despite the mighty din you can pick out the murmur of satisfaction in the section when at last the foreman walks over to the switch. Often we are already stumbling over pieces cluttering the platforms, for the lights on the machines illuminate only the job which is mounted. But we can't change the established order even in matters less important than lighting. '*This* is for *me*,' I heard the foreman say to someone who wanted to play Prometheus.

All newspaper reports on factories mention the music of the workshops. This indescribable sound is undoubtedly the single strongest impression to strike the outside observer or the casual visitor. The noise of the workshop is loud, but to many workers there is music in it. 'Pista's already turned on the music, he's never bored with it,' said my neighbour in irritation when one of the turners began his recurrent daily shaping process, with its characteristic sound. The machines have even stolen our work songs; I too noticed that the music of the machines helps me to find my rhythm.

Sometimes I dream that if composers listened attentively to this workshop music they would understand sooner than others that all servitude begins here, and that there can be no liberation unless it reaches here. Let them hear the clash of finished steel plates as they fall on top of each other, a rhythm dividing time, piece after piece; let them hear the panting of the cutters, as regular as a metronome; the pentatonic wail of the honing machine; the constant sizzling of the plane grinder's hail of sparks; the ever-deepening scream of the rough-cutting lathes, set to speeds for looting, to which the whirling blades reply in ever higher and higher notes, until the moment the machine stops – only to start again without delay; the clatter of the cranes; the hawking rumble from the millers; the sobbing of the shower of glowing shavings on the safety shield (which is so filthy that you can't see what it's made of); the grating of labourers' shovels as they scrape cooled shavings from the concrete floor; the squeal of jammed milling heads; the banging of pieces dropped on platforms; the jingling of the tracer's pointer and little hammer on the steel table; the hissing of condensed air; the calm of the hooter. They ought to come and hear this music; then at least someone in the factory would get some pleasure out of it.

If my machine breaks down, I take a form signed by the foreman to the service point, in a little hall adjoining ours. The scene is peaceful; I walk past the semi-automatic machines from England and West Germany. Mainly women work here, every minute they take out a finished piece, replace it with a new one and press the starter button. A single qualified worker sets three or four machines to turn out the same few types of work. My contact in maintenance says training these women operators doesn't take more than a quarter of an hour. Their wages are so low that no man would take the job.

What I know from other parts of the factory is only from hearsay. Articles in the factory journal, service notes, information about rewards, press reports, are all much of a muchness; the bosses tell us little. Neither do the reluctant anecdotes provided by old workers.

Assembly workers, it is always said, can't have bad hearts. In the frenzy at the end of the year when the conveyor belt is speeded up, they assemble with ten-kilo hammers. 'At such times,' someone says, 'they pass even defective pieces and hammer them straight into the machines.'

Between our hall and the entrance to the factory is the painters' workshop. Their protective masks dangle from their belts; they spray on the stifling toxic paint without wearing them. They, too, are on piece-rates. Their foreman is really 'kind': since he knows that the masks hold up work, he turns a blind eye to the fact that they don't wear them, despite the strict regulations; when one of the big bosses comes along, he warns them himself.

On the testing rack, finished tractors circle and drone unceasingly; there are always a few young apprentices on their way between shops, gazing at the break-neck manoeuvres.

I am not the only one who knows little about the factory. Even the old-timers know virtually nothing. They aren't even interested. 'I'm happy to get home and be out of the place at last' is more or less what everyone says. Many of them travel for several hours a day, and we spend more than eight hours in the factory, even when we aren't doing overtime.

At the start and at the finish of work: the gates, the changing-room; the changing-room, the gates.

In the morning, a mass of men with bleary eyes and hang-dog expressions stream through the security grids. In a great many stomachs there is already the heat of alcohol. The cafes open at 5.30; there is a bar and a private drinks stall between the tram station and the factory. A bad night, early morning stomach pains . . . and they have a new client, who soon makes a habit of it. After work we feel that we owe our clean, desiccated bodies a bottle of beer before going home. We drink them standing up, straight out of the bottle; there's no point in taking a glass; besides they don't rinse them properly.

At the gates, we show our factory cards, with our photos and work numbers: the first three figures are for the section; the last three for the individual. There are two kinds of identity cards, one for workers, another for administrative staff. As for the senior technicians, the security officers know them on sight and don't often make the mistake of asking to check their bags when they are leaving; and even if one of them should not recognize them, he can guess who they are from their busy walk and the brief-case under their arms. The top bosses are saluted, even though this is not prescribed by the regulations.

A worker can count on being searched if his bag is not completely open when he goes past the security guard. From time to time random spot-checks mean a body search. We go into a special cubicle, one by one. A guard examines our bag, another frisks our person, and a third blocks the way out: he's said to be covering. This is what we call a 'raid'. 'Shit! They never raid at three,' says a low voice in front of me in the queue. (The bosses, technicians, and clerks, who start later than we do, leave at 3 o'clock.) 'Speed up, you jailers,' someone else mutters to himself.

In the changing-room, a play in three acts. Before the morning shift, gestures of fatigue. The dank, oily overalls send cold shivers across the skin. The lockers are so narrow that a man could not get into them even sideways. Inside each one there's an iron clothes-hanger and the cockroaches, which we are always squashing but which return every morning: the smell of used oil seems to attract them. Conversations, sharpened by acid, grim humour; anecdotes told to encourage oneself. Well-worn jokes – always the same: 'Hello! Your cockroach has come over to visit me again. Why don't you feed him yourself.' Or, 'Pay day soon! And I haven't managed to spend the last lot.' Thin laughter. Someone else takes him up: 'Then you're really in trouble – because they're going to put up everybody's pay, up like this,' and he repeats a well-worn gag throwing an envelope high into the air.

Someone had been away sick for three days. He was baited by the others: why had he turned out when he was hardly capable of standing up – in fact he didn't look particularly well. 'I couldn't help it,' he said, 'I just had to come. My insatiable lust for work will lead me to my grave.' Amazed, I looked around at the others: they were actually laughing. That, too, was supposed to be a joke. But laughter is a technique – a technique which helps you to get by – and who would throw sand in the machine? At ten to six everyone is standing at his place.

At 2 o'clock the scene is more colourful: those who are arriving are much the same as we were in the morning. But we mix with them: and we try to get into the changing-room a few minutes before the siren sounds. The atmosphere relaxes; old and young alike needle each other, flick out with towels and fool around. Strip those blues! Then the shower – the highpoint of the day; after that, off home, but even in the tram tiredness returns to wrap itself around our shoulders. Heavy, heartless male-chauvinist jokes – the sort favoured by the drinking crowd. Sullen murmurs from those just arriving. Those who are leaving salute ironically one who turns up a bit late; before he gets to his place he'll have been asked three times, 'Been put on night shift, then?' No reply. Someone shouts across the changing-room, 'He can afford to be late. He's the owner of the factory!' Someone else answers, 'Yes, but he doesn't pick up the profits, does he?' There are too few benches; but they also get in the way. There's not enough space between the lockers. 'At the double!' someone shouts, imitating a sergeant-major. At exactly 2 o'clock several of us are already in front of the checking-out clock, dressed, warmed by the shower. The moment the hand touches 2 we start to punch our cards, one after another, non-stop, until the clock almost comes away from the wall. The afternoon shift is already working. As a form of encouragement, some shout at their mates as they go, 'Get on!' or 'Work, slave!'

In the evening, the changing-room belongs to those who are leaving. There are no new arrivals to spoil the mood. The shortage of man-power doesn't allow three shifts. At night, there's only those doing overtime. Little by little, silence falls across the workshop. The calm of the workshops lends a heightened peace to the gaiety of the showers. There's no need to hurry: at home supper and bed wait.

During work, there's a single pause of twenty minutes. At 9 a.m. (or at 5.30 in the afternoon) the siren sounds. We eat. Piece-rate workers can eat when their work allows them to. But it's the custom to stop the machines for 'breakfast', whether you've eaten in advance or not. The older ones think that there's something very wrong with those who continue to work, intoxicated by loot. The inspectors can eat when they like: they've got the time. They deliberately leave their papers all over their tables. But even if they left their tables free, there still wouldn't be enough of them, and anyway there are almost no chairs. The tool-box makes do for a table, the factory magazine for a table-cloth. We change them once a fortnight, when the new edition comes out. The menu: bread, sausage, lard, gherkins, bacon, and cheap cold meats. Occasionally, home-cured pork: quite a few of those who live out of town keep pigs.

There's no running water in the section. This always comes up at every production meeting, but nothing ever changes. Some fill empty beer bottles in the maintenance shop, where there is a tap; others get by with the stale mineral water. We need water only for drinking; we use the cooling liquid, which looks a bit like milk, to clean our hands before eating; water doesn't remove the filth. Everyone has his own 'soap'. It's made once a month from sawdust and the paste used to mix the cooling liquid. We rub our hands repeatedly with this coarse, raw substance, then dry them on packing fibre. This gives an unmistakable flavour to everything we eat.

At 9.20, the siren gives out its signal again. Each has his self-respect, no one runs to the machines. But, by 9.30, the rhythm is back to normal.

In summer, during the afternoon shift, the younger ones don't eat in the section. In front of the building, a weedy patch of grass has sprung up on the ruins of an old factory site. We sit outside, among heaps of rusting pieces which await their destiny. The sun shines. From here the siren can't be heard, but we know that it has already blurted out its signal. We allow ourselves a little loss.

We see the foreman coming, looking for us. To him, each of his steps is a reproach. But we don't move until he reaches us. Our work won't go away. No one will do it in our place.

The Trial of Miklós Haraszti for writing this book*

First hearing, 15–16 October 1973

This report of the public trial of Miklós Haraszti was produced by a person who was present.

Note-taking and the recording of the evidence were forbidden, and quotations are accordingly not verbatim. There may be minor inaccuracies and mistakes in dates, but the greatest care has been taken to preserve objectivity.

The morning of the first day, 15 October, was devoted to the examination of the accused. The President of the Court, Mrs Tóth, read the indictment.

The charge against Miklós Haraszti was incitement to subversion; i.e. he was accused of having written a book likely to stimulate hatred of the State and of having distributed it in several copies.

Miklós Haraszti worked on the shop-floor of a factory, and wrote a book under contract with the publishers Magvetö (Sower) describing what he had seen in the factory. According to the indictment, the book, *Piece-Rates*, claims that the situation of the workers is comparable to that of the natives in the first decades of the colonial era, and that the Party's economic and trade-union officials force the workers to accept ever more arduous schedules in order to get extra income for themselves without working.

The indictment goes on to say that Miklós Haraszti falsified the facts and generalized on the basis of this false picture. In support of this claim the indictment adduces quotations from the book.

The prosecutor, Mr Galambos, made changes in the text of the indictment. He corrected inaccurate quotations and asked that the word 'work', wherever it occurred, should

*This transcript is translated from the version which appeared in *Les Temps Modernes*, August–September 1974, with reference to the version that appeared in *Index*, December 1973 (which preceded the final sentencing).

be placed in quotation marks, since the publication in question was not a literary work but a libellous pamphlet.

The defendant also asked for alterations to the text because it contained distorted quotations.

The Preside..t assured him that he would be able to talk about these later, and that for the present he should say whether or not he had understood the indictment and whether he regarded himself as guilty.

Miklós Haraszti: I have understood the conclusions of the indictment and the penalty it seeks to impose on me, but I do not understand the indictment with regard to its content. The indictment contains quotations which I shall show to be distorted. The indictment does not interpret these quotations, and does not indicate the expressions likely to arouse hatred of the civil order or the institutions which would be concerned.

The indictment contains one reference to the State as such, but the sections of the Penal Code dealing with subversion do not mention the State. They stipulate that incitement to subversion is an act likely to provoke hatred of the civil order, the Constitution or fundamental institutions.

President: Say whether you regard yourself as guilty.

Miklós Haraszti: No, I do not regard myself as guilty in any respect.

In reply, the President recalled that the prosecutor had already initiated police investigations concerning Miklós Haraszti before the present case. Miklós Haraszti argued that the cases referred to by the President were an example of the police exceeding their powers, and constituted an intervention by the police in cultural life.

The President then questioned Haraszti about the date on which the book had been reproduced, the number of copies made, when the contract had been signed with the publishers, the people to whom the defendant had shown the manuscript, and the dates on which he had done so.

Miklós Haraszti: I am amazed at this procedure. It is

clear that the fact of typing nine copies of a book and showing it to others would not be described as criminal if the
prosecutor did not regard its content as subversive.

Detailing the circumstances of the book's distribution
just mentioned might seem to clarify the situation, whereas
in fact the essence remains obscured. The first requirement
is to prove that the book is subversive. There is also an
even more important general issue, namely, whether it
is lawful to prevent the publication of a manuscript by
arresting its author [the indictment revealed that Miklós
Haraszti was held in custody for a fortnight] and initiating
criminal proceedings. This is by no means clear, even
in the case of a book rejected by all the publishing institutions. In my case, the journal *Szociológia* had already accepted
lengthy extracts from the book for publication.

President: You will have an opportunity to talk about that
later. Answer the questions put to you.

Miklós Haraszti: I am bringing up these points so that the
official record will contain a true account of these facts, which
are, I repeat, of minor importance. I wish to stress that the
charge of incitement to subversion has not yet been proved.

In answer to questions, Miklós Haraszti stated that he
had written the book at the end of 1972 and had had two
sets of copies typed, nine copies in all. In between the
typing of the two sets he had altered the manuscript, after
consultation with people he had asked to read it.

Haraszti explained that he had restricted sight of the
manuscript to three categories of people:

(a) sociologists;
(b) writers, for their professional opinions;
(c) artist friends of his.

At this point the President invited him to give his view
of the indictment. This was a difficult task, since he was
interrupted several times. He appealed to the bench to
allow him to finish at least a sentence. The interruptions
and exchanges lasted about forty minutes. What follows
is a summary of this part of the examination.

Miklós Haraszti: My aim was to produce a constructive

critique. I described the situation in the shop faithfully, without making generalizations from it to the industry or the country as a whole. Certainly I criticized piece-work, but this is not a fundamental socialist institution. It is not a socialist institution at all; it is a capitalist institution. The main aim of a socialist strategy in this field is to eliminate piece-work. More generally, the task of any art which regards itself as socialist is to reveal reality and criticize its negative aspects. Such criticism should not be labelled criminal.

President: In Hungary, proceedings in court are based on the indictment. You ought to know that. Restrict yourself to matters mentioned in the indictment.

For example, why do you say that you have no intention of making general statements when you do not even name the factory you discuss in your book?

Miklós Haraszti: One of the characteristics of sociology is precisely this, that it does not specifically mention the place of the investigation. Nevertheless, there is a whole series of details given in the book which prove that it is about a specific shop and a specific factory. I also described the appearance and situation of the factory in a way which leaves no room for doubt.

[In this connection, the defence asked for a properly published and available sociological study to be included in the evidence. It dealt with a similar case in which the opinions attributed to the workers are every bit as hostile as those which are the basis of the charge against Miklós Haraszti.]

It follows that:

1. It is false to say that I generalize, although generalization from particulars is an operation of formal logic. To prove this, it would be sufficient to indicate the passages which present this situation as general. The indictment does not do this at all, but simply states that I make generalizations.

2. It is equally false to say that I falsify reality. The indictment does not even attempt to disprove what I say in the book.

President: It is not the prosecution's task to deny; its task is to prove.

Miklós Haraszti: In that case it should prove that what I have written is false, since this is what it claims.

3. The quotations in the indictment are distorted and out of context. Whole sets of notes are just omitted, and opinions I quote are simply attributed to me. One example: I am said to hold the opinion of a worker who said that the union is a paid enemy.

President: But you share this opinion, don't you?

Miklós Haraszti: In the first place, I am not here because of my opinions, but because of what I have written. Secondly, the issue is not the role of the unions, but the opinions certain workers have of them. These are what I quoted.

President: You claim that the quotations are distorted. That is false. I have personally compared the indictment with your manuscript. Perhaps I know your book better than you.

Miklós Haraszti: In that case you will no doubt agree with me. It has been said, for example, that I compare the situation of factory workers with that of the natives at the beginning of the colonial period. It is enough to read the sentences which surround these quotations to see that I do not say that their situation is identical – that would be absurd. I am talking about a psychological phenomenon. The natives gave away their lands, their property, for trinkets. They only felt cheated when they did not receive the promised 'jewels'. I found that workers in a factory where work was paid at piece-rates found this form of payment natural, and were only scandalized by minor abuses.

That is all, and I recorded it faithfully.

President: There's no need to read all that. Restrict yourself to indicating the pages, paragraphs and lines in question. Read the words which you say are missing. We will take note of them.

This was done. The public made little of it. The defendant then asked for the acceptance as evidence of articles on piece-work and workers' language which had appeared in the Party daily and in a weekly review, and an article by Lenin on trade unions. He noted that the Red Star Tractor Factory referred to in the book had since been absorbed into a larger concern because of bankruptcy.

The President interrupted him, saying that these were facts which were well known to everyone.

The defendant replied that the indictment did not mention them. This argument ended the examination.

The impression the public gained, to judge from conversations heard in the corridors during the break, was as follows. The President was trying to prevent the defendant from addressing the public rather than the Court. She was trying to show that Miklós Haraszti was a frivolous person and a third-rate writer. She interrupted him frequently in motherly tones, scolded him and was coaxing and firm at the same time, which could easily be very irritating for the defendant. In spite of this tone, she was correct, because in the end the defendant was able to make his main points. The defence was able to present documents and correct inaccurate quotations in the indictment, even if it was impossible for the public to know the content of these documents and their value as evidence.

The hearing of witnesses began on the afternoon of the 15th, and continued into the morning of 16 October. All the witnesses had been called by the prosecution. There were thirteen:

six writers: György Konrád, Miklós Mészöly, István Eörsi, András Nyerges, Tamás Szentjóby (the book was dedicated to him), György Dalos (the first four are very well known)

two journalists: Madame Félix Máriássy and Madame Katalin Imre

two of the country's best-known sociologists, András Hegedüs and Iván Szelényi

two film directors: Péter Bascó and Ágnes Háy (Bascó is one of the best-known Hungarian directors)

a young lawyer, Miss Gabrielle Hajós.

The President of the Court asked the witnesses if they had

realized that the manuscript was unpublishable when they received it, and what they thought of it.

Defence Counsel, Loránd Kaczián, asked them how many copies were required by the Magvetö publishing house, and how many readers the firm normally consulted (from two to eight normally, but in the case of Miklós Haraszti the editor based his opinion on that of a single official reader). Counsel also asked how many copies they made of their writings, whether the opinion of the chairman of the firm, Mr Kardos, was decisive, and if the rejection of a manuscript by a publisher excluded its publication. He also questioned the witnesses about their opinion of the book, since it was clear that the prosecution's intention was to show that:

1. Mr Kardos's opinion had decided the fate of the book; he had found it unpublishable because of its style;

2. the witnesses had received the book after its rejection by the publishers. This proved that Miklós Haraszti's aim was not to consult them, but in fact to circulate the book secretly;

3. the witnesses had told the defendant that the book was subversive, but that had not prevented him from letting other people read it.

The evidence of these witnesses turned out to favour the defendant for the following reasons:

1. Two witnesses who knew Mr Kardos stated that he often changed his mind and had on several occasions published books he had previously rejected and vice versa.

All the writers among the witnesses said that if one publisher turned down a book it could appear under another imprint or in a journal.

Mr Szelényi, who, at the time, was editor in chief of the journal *Szociológia* ('Sociology'), said that he had been on the point of publishing the book and that two sociology readers for the review shared his opinion. He had judged the book entirely publishable, and the only reason they were intending to publish only extracts was that they were a journal and not book publishers. It was a problem of space. He was on the point of publishing the chapters analysing the consequences of piece-work and the sections dealing with the social organization of the factory. He had found the passages criticized perfectly acceptable in their context. He had not submitted his proposal to the editorial board because Miklós Haraszti had meanwhile been arrested and he did not want to impede the investigation.

2. Some witnesses had received the manuscript before Mr Kardos's rejection, others after, and others could not remember when.

3. None of the witnesses had found it subversive (one had not read it), even the two who did not like the book.

In reply to Counsel's questions, the writers explained that they had their work typed in between six and sixteen copies. This was, apparently, quite usual. They all asked the opinions of several people on their work.

Konrád: It is one of the finest products of Hungarian sociological writing.

Mészöly: What impresses me is the way the analysis is not performed from outside: it is a feat of vivisection. The subject is approached with great honesty by means of a combination of literary skill and intellectual analysis.

Eörsi: From the literary point of view, I found the book very well written. I was impressed by its structure, its documentary form and also the author's intentions.

Nyerges: The strictly descriptive part is correct, but when the author evaluates the facts he describes, it sometimes gets boring.

Hegedüs: It is a constructive book, moderate in its quotations and in its reproduction of the workers' views on the negative effects of piece-work. We find much similar material in our sociological studies.

Szelényi: The book contains no scientific novelties. The phenomena with which the analysis deals have been described in sociological publications, but the literary and sociographic presentation is of great interest. The findings coincide with the experience of Hungarian sociology.

Máriássy: I found the book naive, but I was impressed by its literary qualities.

When the witnesses had been heard, the President opened the presentation of the evidence.

The prosecutor had nothing to add to the evidence presented in the indictment. Defence Counsel stated that the opinion of the typewriter expert was mistaken. The expert had claimed that the last five copies had been typed on an electric typewriter, but the defence was in a position to produce the manual machine on which the copies had been typed. Defence Counsel also announced his intention of calling sociological and literary experts. His motive in this was not known, but probably had to do with the examination of the accuracy of the book's findings or the interpretation of the quotations attacked, in context.

The President adjourned the hearing.

It was generally expected that after the adjournment the President would read the additional documents submitted by the defence and take a decision on the problem of the experts. But, after the break, she adjourned the trial and announced that the case would be returned to the prosecutor for further information to be obtained. The case, she said, had not been fully explained.

The supplementary investigation would cover:

1. the habits of the publishers concerned, the number of readers used, etc.;

2. the matter of the typewriter expert – the question of the copies;

3. the matter of the copy confiscated on the Yugoslav frontier.

Second hearing, 10–11 January 1974

The trial reopened on 10 January at 9 a.m. The attendance in court was as large as in October, about sixty people. They included about thirty young people, student types, fifteen or so lawyers and various plain-clothes policemen.

The protagonists were the same: Mrs Tóth, the President of the Court, who was assisted by two people's judges, a lady and a gentleman who maintained an utter silence throughout the whole length of the trial; the prosecutor, Mr Galambos, who had been very reserved until now, but was to make a violent closing speech; the defence counsel, Mr Kaczián, who knew the case thoroughly and put forward relevant arguments; and the defendant, Miklós Haraszti.

The results of the supplementary investigation were more or less nil. The typewriter expert admitted his mistake.

The tractor factory referred to in the book stated, by letter, that Miklós Haraszti had in fact worked there as a skilled worker.

The managing director of the publishers stated that he normally asked for the opinions of two readers on manuscripts submitted, but in the present case he himself could be regarded as the second reader.

The President then declared the 'presentation of evidence' closed. Miklós Haraszti asked her to read the documents submitted by the defence. After a break of a quarter of an hour, the President gave a vague explanation of the content of one of the documents and refused to read the others. The Court was obviously embarrassed, but it was not clear exactly why.

Nothing now remained but the closing speeches for prosecution and defence, then the defendant's statement, and the judgement, with its reasons. These are given below, but once again not verbatim.

The Prosecutor's Closing Speech

I do not wish to spend much time on the manuscript, but I must point out that what we are dealing with is in no sense a work of literature, but a libellous pamphlet likely to arouse hatred of the civil order.

The pamphlet deals with the situation of workers at the Red Star Tractor Factory, which it deliberately distorts. The author claims that there is antagonism between the workers at the factory and the management. He claims that the management exploit the workers and systematically humiliate them, with the support of the Party and the unions! He claims that the situation of the workers is identical with that of the proletariat under classical capitalism, that they struggle stubbornly for survival in conditions of great danger for their health, but that their struggle has no chance of even temporary success.

This pamphlet distorts the real situation. It rests on the thesis of the identification of the situation of the Hungarian workers with that of the natives of the beginning of the colonial period. This pamphlet alleges that the unions are 'paid enemies', alien to the interests of the working class.

The opinions of the witnesses are not conclusive in the matter of determining the existence of the crime of incitement to subversion. It is not necessary for hatred of the State actually to be aroused, but merely that the act should be capable of arousing hatred. It follows from this that the calling of experts would serve no purpose, since the problem before us is not sociological or literary, but purely legal.

As for the documents submitted by the defence, they are works of sociology, and contain positive and negative evaluations of phenomena. The manuscript entitled *Piece-Rates* is one-sided, and is not a work of sociology.

We must, and I emphasize this, take into account the whole attitude and activity of Miklós Haraszti, of which the pamphlet before us is the logical extension. I would remind you that Haraszti has twice been the object of proceedings for expressing political opinions hostile to the State. On the second occasion, he received a warning under Paragraph 60 of the Penal Code.

Already, at that time, he had committed a serious offence, but in view of his age the investigating authority had gone no further than a warning. But this warning had no effect, and the pamphlet reflects the whole of the accused's ideology, past and present. There can therefore be no doubt that his intention was to arouse hatred of the State.

We have heard references in court to artistic freedom. There can be no question but that our society fully guarantees the exercise of artistic freedoms. Nevertheless, we must condemn with all the force at our command those who, under the banner of freedom, deliberately slander the institutions of the Hungarian People's Republic. We must condemn them in the interests of the very workers whom the defendant would have us regard as 'exploited'.

In determining the extent of guilt, it must be emphasized that this type of offence is very dangerous to society. The judgement should deter those who share the accused's opinions from slandering the People's Republic of Hungary while using artistic freedom as a pretext.

Under Paragraph 27 of the Penal Code, the penalty for the acts committed by the accused is a term of imprisonment. In addition I ask that the documents should be confiscated and that the defendant should pay the costs of the case.

Defence Counsel's Final Speech

The defence and the prosecution have the same aim, the safeguarding of legality. The prosecution is based on the belief that the attitude of the defendant constitutes a threat to society.

The defence bases its case on the belief that society would be threatened if the courts extended the area of crimes against the State in such a way as to use the resources of the Penal Code in areas with which it has no concern. I say again, the aim of the prosecution and the defence is the same, but, this apart, their cases diverge completely.

Miklós Haraszti has committed no crime, and should be acquitted.

In its judgement the court should express the view that our cultural life is sufficiently solid to evaluate the work of writers without the assistance of the legal authorities.

According to the prosecution, after the publisher had rejected his manuscript the author should have destroyed it. And perhaps that would not have been enough, since the prosecution attacks Miklós Haraszti for allowing the manuscript to be read before its rejection by the publishers. If a single rejection were to have such an effect on authors, half the works now read would have been destroyed and the other half would not even have been written because the authors would have been discouraged in advance.

Furthermore, the journal *Szociológia* has stated that the work was publishable. Who can say that corrections would not have been made, possibly to the very phrases quoted by the indictment.

In other words, normal practice leaves authors themselves, with the assistance of editors and of their colleagues, to carry out the regulatory task which it is now proposed to assign to the criminal law.

The defence would be embarrassed if the author had circulated his work among people incapable of giving him an expert opinion, for example inexperienced students, or indeed the workers of the Red Star factory – their reaction to his book would have been less restrained. Fortunately our cultural life is not a bankrupt factory. We have a healthy artistic community.

The defence makes no secret of its anxiety that the legal authorities saw a danger of an underground literature circulating in manuscript. The harmony established between central government and cultural life excludes this danger.

The charge of illegal circulation and subversion is untenable because the defendant could not have supposed that the people who read his book could be subverted.

At the beginning of these proceedings I knew the book only by hearsay and from the quotations included in the indictment. Since, thanks to the loyalty of the court, I have been able to read the whole work. I saw the sections cited in the indictment. However, I had the impression that I was reading something totally different.

The civil order appears in the work only as a point of reference. Miklós Haraszti was trying to find ways of transforming the deplorable structures of the factory, from a socialist viewpoint. It is true that the book may call in question local leaders. The indictment says that this was not a specific factory. In fact, the book not only says in so many words that it was a real factory, but even adds that it was a factory in which administrative intervention by the government proved unavoidable.

The indictment claims that the book falsifies reality.

It is a claim which might be made. Once made, however, it has to be proved before this court, and no attempt to do this has been made. I ask the court to acquit the defendant because he is innocent.

The Defendant's Statement

I shall not repeat what I said about the indictment three months ago, in spite of the fact that the record of the trial does not reproduce even in outline my explanation of the real meaning of the quotations from the book which appear in the indictment. Furthermore, I received the record only yesterday.

The interesting point about the charge of clandestine circulation is the evidence of the witnesses. This shows that it is customary to have duplicated manuscripts read by acquaintances. It follows that the aim of the police and prosecutor was to secure a condemnation of citizens who write or read works which are not officially published.

The evidence presented by the prosecution for the charge of incitement to subversion amounts to a series of quotations totalling less than two pages. Even if the quotations were accurate, they would constitute proof only if a real situation had been distorted and fundamental institutions insulted. Truth is not an incitement to subversion. If a work does not lie and does not even mention the institutions referred to in the Constitution, it cannot be an incitement to subversion, even if the relevant paragraph of our Penal Code does allow a terrifying freedom of interpretation.

The prosecution could have called experts to show that I am lying, but it was the defence who asked leave to call experts. This request was refused, first by the police, then by the prosecutor, and finally by the court, so that the defence was deprived of its last chance of proving its case.

The prosecution has no evidence and no experts. Why then does it want to have me convicted? We have heard the reason in this court. It is because it regards as subversive, not so much the book, but rather an attitude, an opinion. The prosecution is seeking the condemnation of the attitude which wants to expose reality, the belief that our society contains conflicts, the belief that it is the duty and the interest of socialism to bring these conflicts to light. The prosecution bases'its case on a fiction, on the myth of a society without conflicts. If reality looks like giving the lie to this myth, it threatens it with several years' imprisonment. Acceptance of this view would not eliminate conflicts. On the contrary, it would delay their solution.

In the present case, this means that the retention of piecework, this institution created by capitalism, may serve the interests of certain social groups, but not those of the majority. Just as the non-revelation of the facts and the punishment of those who reveal the realities can only serve particular interests.

If the court were to accept the point of view of the prosecution, it would be defending the interests of a very clearly definable sociological group. Such a verdict would also have the effect of formalizing the intervention of the police in cultural life and would give them the right to determine the development of our culture.

This raises another question. Is it proper for the police to carry out a series of dawn raids to seize copies of a manuscript in the course of publication? Is it proper for them to confiscate manuscripts and personal notes which have nothing to do with the case? The police held me in custody for three days. Then they charged me, and throughout the period of my detention denied me the opportunity of getting in touch with my mother or my lawyer. I was forced to protest against these methods by going on hunger strike. I was not released until I had been on hunger strike for a fortnight.

I ask the court to acquit me.

The Verdict delivered by Mrs Tóth

The Budapest Court sentences Miklós Haraszti to eight months' imprisonment, suspended for three years. If during that period he is convicted of a violation of the laws the present sentence will be carried out.

In addition, the court orders the nine copies of the manuscript *Darabbér* to be confiscated, and orders that the defendant shall pay the costs of the hearing, which amount to 9,600 forints.

The public then resumed their seats, and the President turned to the reasons for the verdict.

President: The court considered the question whether the manuscript deals with a single factory or not, and found that it does not. There are passages in which the defendant attacks all managers, all those whom he calls 'them'. He even claims, and I quote the manuscript, that the designation 'them' goes beyond the walls of the factory and refers to all those who take decisions, from top leaders to football referees, to all who hold power and their like. This is only one of many passages in this vein.

The author also gives a false picture of reality. For example, he claims that the workers who work on two machines at a time, instead of one as before, can be compared to the natives in the early days of the colonial period.

In settling the question whether or not the defendant realized that his manuscript might arouse hatred of the civil order, the opinions of the witnesses are only of limited value. We know that as early as 1970 the defendant maintained the view that there exists in Hungary a privileged class which is out of touch with the problems of the working class. He had received a warning from the authorities, and therefore knew very well what he was doing.

On the question of the circulation of the manuscript, it is true that the number of copies typed was not greater than is usual, but the number of copies in existence and the number of readers involved are themselves enough to confirm the gravity of the offence.

For this offence the Penal Code stipulates a penalty of between two and eight years' imprisonment. The Court reached its decision on the basis of the paragraph dealing with attenuating circumstances, having regard to the following points:

1. Except for one or two people, Miklós Haraszti showed the manuscript to close acquaintances who have similar

ideas to his own, and this reduced the anti-social force of his action.

2. Miklós Haraszti tried to have his manuscript published legally, although it is also true that this is now standard practice among those who maintain an oppositional view of Hungarian society.

However, these constitute attenuating circumstances, and the Court has decided that its aim can be achieved without the imprisonment of the defendant.

The other parts of the verdict follow directly from the provisions of the law, and so require no special explanation.